A Precious Place

A naturalist explores New Jersey
By Don Freiday

Drawings by Cathy Freiday
Foreword by Pete Dunne

First edition

Published in the United States of America
by
D.H Moreau Books, P.O. Box 32,
Flemington, N.J. 08822-0032.

Edited by Nicholas DiGiovanni
Design by Rachel Ratkowski

Dedication

For Rebecca, Tim, Don and Cathy.

Winter . . . . •**Page 1**

Spring . . . . •**Page 45**

Summer . . . . •**Page 83**

Fall . . . . •**Page 121**

Preface

This book is a compilation of essays on nature written between 1986 and 1996. Most of the essays were first published in New Jersey Audubon magazine or the Hunterdon County Democrat newspapers, although many have been substantially revised. One or two are new to print.

The book's subject matter ranges widely but stays mostly in one place: New Jersey, especially Hunterdon County, where I have lived and worked for most of this time. Having also travelled some over these 10 years, I make no apology for that fact, but venture to say the material here is relevant to anyone east of the Mississippi with an interest in nature.

If there is inspiration in this book, it comes from the subject matter and from the company of many people. In particular I'd like to thank: Meredith Allen, Chris Aquila, Gene Berliner, Cathy Blumig, Fletch Coleman, Pete Dunne, the late Dr. Paul Fluck, Donald R. Freiday, Rich Kane, Pam Thier, Len Wolgast, Dave Womer, Nancy Yard; all the participants in my classes and field trips, in particular my birding trips and Environmental Camp; the staff of the New Jersey Audubon Society; the Hunterdon County Democrat, and the Hunterdon County Park System.

Cathy Freiday created the pen-and-ink drawings for the book, and also tolerates her husband's frequent absences in the field. Don, Tim and Rebecca Freiday inspire me like no others can or will.

Perhaps my greatest joy has been sharing nature through the seasons with these fine people. I invite the reader to join us.

Don Freiday
September 1997

Foreword

The best advice I can offer anyone reading this line is – don't. Skip this foreword. Turn the page. Start savoring the text of Don Freiday's collection of essays. Once you start, you won't stop. Once you've finished, you'll have a new favorite nature writer.

I'm serious about this. Stop reading this foreword. Read this book! You'll discover, as I have, that this Hunterdon County naturalist and New Jersey native is one of the most refreshing writers to come along in a long time. I say this not because Don and I are friends – although we are. I say this because my praise is demonstrably true. The evidence rests in your hands.

So get on with it. Don't waste precious time reading this. Don't...

Think what it means to a veteran writer like myself to "discover" an up-and-coming star like Don. I've known him for more than a decade, known him since his early days as a naturalist at the New Jersey Audubon Society's Scherman-Hoffman Sanctuary (before his skills propelled him to his current post of chief naturalist for the Hunterdon County Park System). During this time, I've come to admire his storehouse of knowledge, his acumen, his passion for all that is wild and beautiful, his philosophical grounding in the natural world that he has shared with thousands of readers of New Jersey Audubon magazine and the Hunterdon County Democrat.

I confess that I have even come to envy Don's ability to bridge the gap between people and nature with words. Any naturalist worthy of the name can expound upon the changing seasons ... describe the tree species found in northeastern woodlands ... discuss territoriality, migration, predation – all the basic tenets of the natural world.

Very few can forge these ideas into concepts and stories that come alive in people's minds.

But Don can. And you will see that he can. As soon as you take my advice. Stop reading this tribute. Start savoring this book.

Wait till you meet Frank, the gutsy catbird with the near-fatal flaw. (Hint, hint ... it's an allegory that questions one of environmental education's guiding principles).

Wait till you read "What the goose thinks." You'll never think of life, death and human responsibility quite the same again.

Wait till you read "The distance," the essay that explores the limits of human perception, and learn why I am so jealous of this essay. I've spent most of my life pushing the limits of bird identification. I've moored my life to that gray border that lies on the far side of an objective lens and this side of conjecture. I've even written books on the subject! But until Don succeeded in binding this Never-Never Land with that single catalytic phrase – "The distance" – I never really understood what I was doing ... or why.

Boy, am I jealous. Boy, are you wasting your time not cutting the corner on this foreword and jumping into this book.

But if, for reasons of perversity or politeness to authors, you continue to read these words, then let me take the opportunity to introduce Cathy Freiday, Don's perfect half. She's not only supportive, she's talented. What Don can do with words, Cathy can bring to life with an artist's hand. So, hand in hand, Don and Cathy have crafted a book to match their life together.

The beneficiary is you.

Still reading, aren't you? Well, then my duty to you as a reader – and to Don and Cathy – is clear. I'm going to stop writing, so you can come to discover the natural wonders of a wonderful state, a talented writer, and their synthesis which is this book.

Don't be deceived. I'm not shutting down my word processor for your sake (or Don's). My motive is simple and selfish. As soon as I stop writing, I'm free to follow my own good advice – the advice you have thus far ignored – and read Don's collection again.

Skipping only those parts that make the writer in me jealous.

PETE DUNNE
Vice President
New Jersey Audubon Society

Winter

The Christmas Owl

Winter

"Good luck, Frank"

I almost missed out on what Frank had to teach. What he had to teach was gritty and emotional. Grit I can understand, but emotion? I am not so emotional. I almost let Frank die.

I first noticed Frank on Nov. 10, according to my field notes. I first noticed him that day, but I may very well have seen him a hundred times before. Frank lived in the thickets along my driveway.

It took until Nov. 10 to notice him because Frank was a catbird, and birders in New Jersey pay about as much attention to catbirds as parkway drivers do to speed limit signs.

Catbirds suffer the misfortune of being abundant, easy to see and relatively drab to look at.

But a catbird on Nov. 10 begins to take on special significance: Will it make it until the count? That is, the Christmas Bird Count.

Catbirds generally are not supposed to winter in New Jersey, although a few do every year. In fact, catbirds winter as far south as Panama and the Caribbean. They are one of the "half-hardy" species, able to survive well north of their normal winter range, if the weather is not too severe.

Frank made it to the count – past the count, in fact – until a twist in the weather, a twist of fate and a twist of my arm provided by my wife brought Frank into our home.

I had theorized for a number of years that catbirds wintering in New Jersey were just genetic anomalies, anomalies that might become the rule some century when the warming climate and declining habitat for migrants made staying north a better bet for surviving.

There are, of course, alternative theories. A bird-bander friend of mine suggested that the catbirds, orioles and other half-hardies stay north because they are injured and cannot migrate. He studied bird vision, and believes many lingerers might have scratched corneas or other vision problems.

I never really considered the plight of each individual lingerer – until Frank. Scientists tend to consider species of animals, or populations, but not the statistically insignificant individual. Let the least bit of emotion enter your scientific pursuits, and before you know it people will be calling you a bunny hugger or start questioning your conclusions. I suppose you could compare this school of thought with that of psychologists, whose profession does not allow them to become emotionally attached to their patients.

But consider this: You are a bird accustomed to plenty of insects and soft berries to feed you, plenty of foliage to hide you and plenty of other birds to draw the attention of predators. As October fades into November into December, the things you are accustomed to finding easily cannot be found at all. Winter opens the sheltering thicket to claw and tooth and talon. Whatever your reasons for staying north, you are now forced to adapt, to do whatever it takes to survive. You adapt or you die.

Beginning in December, I made a daily effort to see Frank. Many days I could not find him, even though I knew exactly which bushes he favored. If I saw him at all, I saw him from my truck. Frank seemed very sensitive to anything approaching him on foot. If he flew, he flew low, and always managed to weave his way into the most tangled rosebush imaginable. I never really saw him well.

Frank gave the impression of being a rather exceptional catbird. To be honest, some genuine emotion crept into my asbestos-coated heart when, one January morning, I searched for but could not find him. Asbestos is pretty dangerous stuff, I have since decided. Whether scientifically correct or not, I missed Frank.

Frank's winter brought multiple late snowstorms. While not deep, the snow complicated life for wintering birds. At the time I was most concerned about the woodcock, which had returned only a few days before the last storm and had been displaying within earshot of my home. A snowy ground cover must make it plenty hard, or at least uncomfortable, for a woodcock to find worms in the mud.

Frank the catbird was all but forgotten, missing and presumed dead. So when my wife hurried into the kitchen one morning to report a catbird alive but not moving in the middle of the driveway, I was not a little surprised. I grabbed the nearest coat, and headed for the spot with her.

The middle of the driveway. Of the hundreds of places that bird could have chosen to lay until he died, he chose the middle of the driveway. My driveway.

"Well, he's on his way out, all right. I can hardly believe he's lasted this long." Still the scientist.

The bird lay quite still, his eyes bright and alert, his wings partially fanned. He showed no inclination to flee.

"Aren't we going to do something?" Her words were emphatic puffs of steam in the cold morning. This was not a fair question; she knows well I have little use for capturing and rehabilitating anything wild. Let nature take its course and all that. Sure... and she'd sic the kids on me next.

And there was something else. This catbird (he didn't have a name yet; we christened him "Frank" after he lived with us long enough to earn the name of a spastic desert lizard in one of my kids' videos) had touched a nerve in me. He sure wanted to live. I couldn't quite see letting him die with sweet, warm spring so near. Imagine how that bird was waiting for spring. Imagine how he felt when, after a warm evening when the woodcock were calling, he awoke to a cold, white morning.

Anyhow, life's too short to waste as a scientist.

I bent down to pick the bird up. To my surprise, he fluttered off, although he was apparently too weak to get off the ground. And then I noticed something else. His right leg poked out to the side, at an impossible angle – an impossible angle, because his wing hit it every time he flapped, making flying more than a foot off the ground impossible and, I soon found out, making the simple act of taking a perch impossible.

But the bad leg didn't keep him from worming his way into a rosebush. As I lay on my belly in the snow trying to reach him, cutting my fingers on the thorns, I thought: This bird is about survival. What possibly can drive a bird to keep going for four months of winter while unable to fly well or perch? How could it find food? Or avoid cats, raccoons, foxes, and hawks?

Frank and I were both cold when I finally laid my hand on him. The chill of Frank's body shocked me. Normally, a bird in the hand feels noticeably warm. Frank was also without doubt the thinnest catbird I have ever held, although while bird banding I have handled quite a few. Clearly he needed warmth and food.

Warmth was easy. I cradled him inside my shirt as we walked to the house, and once in the house he probably dreamed he had died and gone to spring.

But what could I feed him? He nibbled without enthusiasm at the bananas and apples I proffered. After bringing him in and showing him to the children, I knew I had to make him live. I had to.

Mealworms. I called work and said without explanation that

I'd be late, then drove the Blazer to a sporting goods store for three dozen meal worms. Mealworms, which are gross-looking beetle larvae to non-fishermen, were the answer, and Frank packed them away like a college student eating pizza. Life grows within when a bird eats from your hand, even if it's only a catbird.

Frank stayed with us for four days, during which time he endured much handling, patting, and a moderately successful but certainly painful attempt by me to re-set his leg. He also devoured several score of meal worms, as well as California strawberries and South American grapes. We released him on a fine warm day after the snow had gone.

"Good luck, Frank," we all said, and we meant it. He sallied gamely into the rose bushes, and gave a little "chuck" call when he landed.

I don't mean to sound unscientific, but that is how catbirds say good-bye.

A winter night

It is 4:30 a.m. and I walk down a quiet farm lane, gravel crunching softly underfoot. The full moon shines, drawing shadow pictures of bare dark trees on the lane. The air smells clean and feels sharp, stinging vaguely on my face. A great-horned owl hoots from some distant place, where no doubt the rabbits have stopped, stock still, to listen, and to not be heard.

I nearly step on a rabbit, out of hearing range for this owl, but crouched very still nonetheless by the side of the road. The rabbit darts off, soundlessly at first on the winter wheat and pattering rapidly on dry leaves when he reaches the woodlot.

Maybe the rabbit is not out of reach for the

great-horned's ears. I am always amazed how far sound carries on a quiet winter night. The woodlot is 200 yards away, and still the rabbit's rapid footfalls bridge the distance between us long after he reaches it. The owl, no doubt, hears much farther than I.

Night sounds in winter are few, which makes them all the more noticeable. When I stop to listen, I can hear the soft scurrying and squeaking noises of what must be white-footed mice moving about in a hedgerow. A distant brook's babbling is not only audible, but loud.

The sounds of the footsteps of night creatures can often be distinguished by their patterns. Deer move rhythmically, but pause often. Rabbits dash and stop. Foxes trot quickly, making rapid footsteps that sometimes pause, sometimes not. Raccoons lumber, as do skunks, making uneven sounds often punctuated by scraping or digging. The skunk's footfalls are softer than the raccoon's.

No insects or frogs call on a frozen night. Soft twitterings or single notes in a thicket are songbirds, possibly disturbed on their night-time roost by my movements, or those of a predator. Songbirds typically spend the cold nights roosting in thickets or evergreens, sometimes huddled together for warmth. A few species will use cavities in trees for roosting.

The whistling snort of a deer startles me as I walk, letting me know my presence has not gone undetected. No doubt it is a doe, sending a warning to her fawns and other nearby deer that a human is about. When an unseen deer snorts a warning, a check of the wind will usually reveal that the deer is downwind, using its keen sense of smell to detect danger. It is unfortunate that humans have lost much of their nasal ability. Undoubtedly we miss many things that deer, dogs and other mammals take for granted.

Our ears certainly miss sounds that wild animals hear with ease. Apparently, the dogs in the house next door find no difficulty in detecting what I think are quiet human steps: mine.

Well, it is almost 6 a.m., time for everyone to wake up anyhow. I step reluctantly down my driveway, musing that I should make a more regular habit of these nighttime winter walks.

Deep snow

Deep in the Blizzard of '96, no pun intended, I sat at the kitchen table with a cup of coffee and my daughter, Rebecca, sagely thinking naturalist thoughts. Mainly I thought that any animal with a lick of sense was holed up in some thicket, burrow, hollow tree or house for the day. Myself included.

Even as I thought that thought (at the same moment, honest!), Rebecca called out: "A fox, a fox! Look! A fox!"

She had been watching the snow through the steamed-up kitchen window. Knowing my daughter, I expected she had seen a drift or swirl of snow shaped like a fox, or a drift, or had with her fingers painted a fox on the steamed-up window. I leisurely pushed my chair back, and leaned around to see where she was looking.

A lovely red fox bounded like a wraith across the drainageway on the east side of the house, and disappeared into the blizzard. So much for sage naturalist thoughts.

I could not and cannot imagine where that fox was going, unless he had developed cabin fever and wanted to see what the snow was doing to everyone else.

In the same way, I wanted to ignore the government-declared state of emergency and go for a drive in my jeep, but 4-foot drifts prevented me from even reaching the road. My explorations would have to wait for clear skies and snow shoes.

How did the blizzard affect wildlife?

Just like for people, one of the most pressing problems for

animals in deep snow is mobility. This is especially true for large, heavy animals like deer.

Snow deeper than 20 inches drastically reduces deer mobility. In poor habitat areas, moving around to feed in deep snow may cost more energy than can be obtained from food. This is not such a problem in good habitat, because deer foods such as shrubs, vines and agricultural crops are readily available.

In 1996, the deer herd also entered the winter in excellent condition, especially because of the heavy acorn crop of the fall, and were well-prepared to withstand an extended period of deep snow.

Deer tend to quickly form beaten paths in deep snow, and stick to them. I found one place where a single, ditch-like trail in the deep snow led from a swampy thicket to a patch of standing corn. The deer obviously had already begun traveling on this single path, back and forth between food and shelter.

Even small, light animals like rabbits move with difficulty if the snow is extremely powdery. The lightest crust, however, will support a rabbit's weight, and only a day after the storm I saw rabbits out and about, hopping gingerly along the surface of the snow.

Come spring, it will be interesting to look for the places where rabbits had gnawed the bark from young trees and rose bushes, and to remember how deep the snow was. Some of these gnawings will be 4 feet off the ground!

Finding a Christmas tree

Rain fell lightly, and bluebirds called plaintively from the nearby hedgerow. The ground squished underfoot, too soggy even to hold the tracks from the deer that no doubt visit some uninvited nightly pruning on this Christmas tree farm.

Soggy though it was, nothing could dampen our kids' spirits as they raced in and out of the rows and rows of conifers on this day after Thanksgiving. Juncoes and white-throated sparrows were flushed from between the rows, twirling and darting across the farm to the safety of several rows of uncut Scotch pine which were too old and too tall to be in much danger from two-legged tree seekers. A long-eared owl probably watched from its vantage there, and I was tempted to go looking for one.

They say traditions are a good thing for a family, and choosing a Christmas tree to bring into our home is something I've done with mine ever since my son was old enough to leave those tiny, muddy work boot footprints all over the seat of the old pick-up. We've wound our way over the years through a series of trucks, homes, and workboots, but every year there is a tree. It's not the same tree, and it's not from the same place, but it's always an adventure finding the right one.

One December, we visited a tree farm near Jutland and brought home a white pine — along with a handful of owl pellets we found under some older, taller trees.

White pines grow natively farther north, and are widely planted. The species wears long, graceful needles in bundles of five, and presents an open-branched appearance.

Many years, we select pre-cut Fraser firs, brought in by tree farmer friends who also happen to be wildlife biologists by profession. The trip to their farm is as much a chance to see their dogs, catch up on hunting stories and talk about what ducks are using their pond as it is to find a tree.

Frasers are great trees, fragrant and persistent in holding their needles. Unfortunately, the range in which Fraser firs grow well is restricted to the mountain slopes of southern Virginia, North Carolina and Tennessee, generally in areas above 4,000 feet. They are not grown locally, which means guilty feelings for an environmentalist because of the fossil fuels burned to bring the trees to New Jersey.

This year and last we opted for locally grown Douglas firs, a western species that adapts well to our climate and soils, and one that does about as well indoors as a Fraser fir. We also get to walk the land a while to look for one, something not to be taken lightly. Last Friday we found a fine tree on a farm in East

Amwell, and a lot more besides.

Many of the trees we looked at housed bird nests, built last spring or summer but not to be used again. Many more trees were flecked with the "whitewash" of bird droppings, revealing the night-time roost site of some house finch, dove, sparrow, or other species. We also found "forms," depressed areas of grass where rabbits rest. A red-tailed hawk cruised over as we paid for the tree, its bulging throat attesting to a recently captured meal.

The bluebirds called, the rain fell, the kids laughed, and already I can't wait to find our tree next year.

Tracks in the snow

Pine cones lay all over the snow. They had not been there five minutes before, when I'd looked out the kitchen window. Now there they were, glaringly obvious on top of the crusted white snow.

Actually, they were not even pine cones. They were spruce cones, Norway spruce cones to be exact. Like so many people, we have a row of tall spruces lining our driveway. Spruce cones do not fall en masse of their own volition, and although I was pretty sure what was going on, I went outside to check.

The first thing I heard was a cone crashing branch to branch as it hurtled 50 feet to the snow. Shortly after, an animal scolded me from the top of the spruce, sounding remarkably like a camera autowinder gone haywire. My analysis had been correct: A red squirrel was cutting off cones and throwing them to the ground, to be cached for later consumption. I had not seen a red squirrel for several days, probably because of continued stormy weather.

Snow is a wonderful thing for a naturalist. To see an animal requires luck, while finding tracks, fallen pine cones, or any other sign is easy with snow on the ground. Careful interpretation of tracks can tell much more about an animal than merely glimpsing the animal itself.

Later that afternoon, I went walking with my kids, looking for tracks and what have you. Of course, deer tracks were everywhere – under the bird feeder, behind the shed and near the pond. Interestingly, a walking deer's foot print is always the mark of the hind foot, for as the animal walks it places its rear hoof exactly where the front one had been.

Tracks laced the meadows. An opossum had wandered up our sledding hill. We could not clearly make out the shape of its feet, but the dragmarks from the skinny tail were a dead giveaway.

An opossum's forefoot has five toes, and looks a little like a raccoon's "hand" print, but the rear foot of an opossum is unique. Each foot has a large "thumb," which points almost opposite from the rest of the fingers, nearly back the way the animal came. The hind feet help the 'possum hang on when it climbs.

Pheasant tracks wandered along the hedgerows, all no doubt from birds recently released by gun clubs. Native pheasants, meaning birds born in the wild, are few and far between in the Northeast. Technically, no American pheasant is native, because the species was originally imported to North America from Asia, by way of England.

Crow tracks mixed with the pheasant tracks. The two can be distinguished by the length of the hind toe. A pheasant has a foot adapted for walking, and so its rear toe is relatively short. The crow, adapted to perch in trees, has a long hind toe to wrap around branches. The pheasants and crows fed on a few shriveled persimmons which had recently fallen from the rough-barked trees adjoining the meadow.

We found some unusual tracks out in the middle of an open area. They were about an inch wide, and ranged from 10 inches to several feet in length. At first I thought they were troughs in the snow made by some rodent as it pushed its way along –

until I looked up. Overhead were power lines, and the tracks had been made by ice falling off the wires.

Winter hawks

Why are some hawks around all year while others migrate? The dead of winter, when you would think any hawk in its right mind would have left town, seems as good a time as any to answer this question.

To say that migration is a complicated phenomenon would be an understatement, but one general principle holds almost all the time: Migration is about food, much more than it is about temperature. Animals go where the food is.

If you are a broad-winged hawk that eats frogs and insects, you will starve in New Jersey in January. On the other hand, if you happen to be a red-tailed hawk, and you want to find small mammals, winter may actually be a better time than summer to do it, because the vegetative cover that hid your summer prey is now gone.

So broad-wingeds go and redtails stay. Insectivorous warblers go while seed-eating sparrows stay. This is bird migration in a nutshell.

But migration is a lot more complicated than that, and individual birds and bird populations adopt different strategies. The redtail offers a good example.

The red-tailed hawk pretty much rules the winter skies; it is the common large hawk. Some of the individual redtails we see hunting along roadsides and field edges in winter are present year round, nesting in woodlots and forest pockets throughout the state. Our winter redtail population is augmented by birds that may have nested in Canada, and have come here only for the winter. These birds will fly back north in February and March.

To make matters even more complicated, some of the redtails that nested in the local woodlots last summer are now to the south of us, and will not return until March.

So what about the return migration in spring? There is indeed a hawk flight in spring, but it is much less concentrated in space and time than fall's southbound flight. Hawks seem to come north in dribs and drabs, spread out over days and over different locations, and a good day of hawk watching in spring would be considered poor in fall.

There are also fewer hawks coming north in spring than went south in fall. At most sites, the bulk of the fall migration is made up of first-year birds, individuals that hatched only the summer before. Most of these individuals will die in migration, or on the wintering grounds.

Migration is the acid test of natural selection, and only the best survive. In some species, for every bird that lives to adulthood as many as nine die before nesting even once.

This should make us appreciate all the more the beauty of a soaring redtail, or of a hunting northern harrier, in the winter sky.

Trees every child should know

Woe is me, at 5 in the morning, sitting in the library at the computer, eyes wandering about the bookshelves, looking for a story to write since none seems to be in my head. The coffee must not be strong enough.

An aged book waits quietly on the shelf, perhaps longing for the time when parents and school teachers, not computers and televisions, controlled how children learned. Its editor named the book "Prose Every Child Should Know."

Three shelves over, four or five tree field guides stand side by side. These are more frequently opened than "Prose Every Child Should Know."

Hmmmm. "Trees Every Child Should Know." Reminds me of something I would read in the Boy Scout manual. Even so, children should know a few trees. Which ones?

Every child should know the elm, for its graceful vaselike

shape and its very hard, virtually unsplittable wood. Every child should know that far fewer elms grace our meadows and streets than in times past. Dutch elm disease reduced the tree to a twig of its former abundance.

Every child should know, or know of, the American chestnut, once the most abundant tree in the eastern forest. Now nearly all the huge American chestnuts are gone, and their progeny languish as stump sprouts under a canopy of oak and tulip poplar.

Let's not become too maudlin. Every child should know the white oak, still common despite the gypsy moths, and a marvelous tree. White oaks are undeniably useful: They make excellent firewood, and the wood is fine for furniture, for tools, and for baskets. The tree is even better alive, because squirrels and deer hold its acorns in the highest esteem, and warblers flock to the spreading branches to feed on the insects there.

Every child should know the shagbark hickory, a tree with a name that describes it. Hickory wood burns longer and hotter than nearly anything else, adds a fine flavor to steak, and is hard enough for a hammer handle. Squirrels devour the tree's large nuts.

My wife, Cathy, just awoke and tells me I ought to get sassafras on the list. Why, I ask? Because sassafras twigs are great for roasting marshmallows. They peel easily, smell fine, aren't sticky, and usually are green enough that they don't ignite. Okay, put sassafras on the list. That's the problem with authority figures - they don't think from a kid's perspective.

What, then, about Christmas trees? Every child should know the difference between, say, an Austrian pine, which will drop needles all over the toys, and a Fraser fir, which will not.

Grouse wilds

The chief value of wilderness may well be its role as a sanctuary for people – from people. Now and then, most of us long to leave the voices, cars, sirens, barking dogs, and the rest of the noise that pollutes the civilized world.

Some time ago, I realized in sorrow that a place truly free of human made sounds does not exist in my home county of Hunterdon, although on a peaceful Sunday morning some of the county's larger forests approach silence.

I needed, one winter day, to listen to the silence for a while, so a trip farther afield was in order. Since Alaska's north slope is somewhat distant for a half-day trek, I journeyed to Waywayanda State Park in extreme northern New Jersey. At Waywayanda, nestled securely in the Highlands of the state, a hiker can penetrate enough forest to escape all but the planes overhead.

Snow blanketed the park's rocky terrain, and crunched under my boots. Tracks were everywhere, weaving shapes and letters onto the landscape. Squirrel tracks... turkey tracks... chipmunk tracks... deer tracks... junco tracks... and something new.

An irregular, close-spaced dotted line wound across the snow-covered trail and into a barberry thicket. The prints resembled the three-toed marks of a wild turkey, but the toes seemed proportionately thicker, and a single track barely spanned 2 inches. What leaves the track of a small, turkey-like bird in deep woods?

Ruffed grouse was the only candidate. Grouse possess a unique adaptation for walking on snow. A fringe of scales develops on their toes in winter, increasing the surface area of their feet and making it easier to walk on soft snow.

Grouse choose to live their lives in the solitude of large tracts of open land – perhaps it is only in such places that they can survive. Like many kinds of wildlife, ruffed grouse are vulnerable to the gamut of human-induced changes to the landscape, from the obvious development and tree-cutting to less obvious but just as threatening impacts.

As open tracts of land shrink, animals like grouse become vulnerable to an array of what might be called human-subsidized predators. These include pets like cats and dogs, which can be very effective predators on wildlife. Some wildlife species themselves are also human-subsidized predators, because they become more abundant in the proximity of man. Raccoons, skunks, blue jays, and crows fall into this category. From cat to crow, human-subsidized predators are more abundant than they would be in a natural system, and can dramatically reduce or eliminate the populations of some other species. Ground-dwelling birds like grouse are especially vulnerable.

Human-subsidized predators are not a problem in the interior of a large park like Waywayanda, and so the place is a prime locale for grouse. Hunterdon's remaining large tracts of forested open space are equally prime. These lands are refuges not only for people, but for wildlife as well.

The Christmas owl

This is about being in the right place at the right time, and it starts with ice skating and ends with an owl.

Between Christmas and New Year's Day, I ice-skated with my kids. It was my first time on skates in at least 10 years. I couldn't find my hockey skates, so I pulled on an old pair of figure skates that didn't fit. Unbelievable blisters were the result.

The day after ice skating I caught a cold, and began coughing up all kinds of yucky stuff. That night, a friend of mine called and asked if I wanted a deer. A fresh road kill, to be precise, that he had found near his place of work. I said sure, why not, we could use the meat, and there was no sense having the deer go to waste, although I am sure the vultures, crows, foxes and other scavengers would disagree about the waste part. My friend assured me the deer was in good shape for being dead.

He brought me the deer the following night, frozen solid. We hung it in the basement to thaw, and the next day I butchered it. Only one hindquarter and the backstraps were salvageable, from a human's point of view, so I was left with most of the carcass to dispose of.

Ordinarily, I would have dragged the carcass to the fields way below the house, where the vultures and foxes could feed on it in peace. This was not an ordinary case, however. The cold was still with me, my feet still hurt from the ice-skating blisters, and I just didn't feel like dragging 60 pounds of mangled deer a quarter mile.

So I headed up the driveway with it, my son, Tim, and dog, Rachel, in tow, to set it out for the scavengers in a small field a short way from the house.

We had made our limping progress about halfway to the field, when I awoke to the fact that a bunch of blue jays were screaming bloody murder in one of the white pines lining the driveway. I said to Tim, "You watch now, pal, I bet there's an owl up here." Blue jays and other small birds will often "mob" an owl or hawk, in an attempt to drive it away.

So I hobbled up to the tree the jays were in and began following each branch from trunk to tip with my eyes, hoping to spot the owl. I started at the top and worked my way down. When I reached the bottom branch, a scant 10 feet up, I began to think I was wrong about the owl.

But I wasn't. He sat calmly perched on the bottom branch. There we were, eye to eye with a saw-whet owl, all 8 inches of it.

Saw-whet owls are the smallest eastern owl, and can be remarkably tame, as this one proved. He looked us over, and then intently ignored the man, boy, dead deer, and wildly circling dog beneath him.

Saw-whet owls are also pretty rare, and they can be real devils for birdwatchers to find, because they are so small, are totally nocturnal, and usually roost in dense conifers or viny tangles. Not a few of my birder friends still need a saw-whet owl for their life lists. This one made a fine Christmas present, and a present it was.

If I had not hurt my feet, gotten a cold, and been stuck with a deer carcass to dispose of that day, I never would have found the saw-whet.

Keeping lists

Along about New Year's Day, most serious birders start thinking pretty hard about their year list. Birders, you see, are often infatuated with lists. The more species on the list, the happier the birder.

There are Life Lists, State Lists, County Lists, Yard Lists, Month Lists, Big Day Lists, Birds Seen from the Car Lists, Birds Seen from the Bathroom Window Lists, and on and on and on.

A year list, as you might guess, tabulates the species found over the course of the year, each species counting as one. Birders think most about the year list near New Year's Day because it is time to count 'em up from last year (and make a last-ditch effort for that missing glaucous gull), and also because it is time to start counting 'em up for next year.

Since I am writing on New Year's Day, the junco at my feeder now is my "year junco," and so are the white-throated sparrows, downy woodpeckers, and house finches "year" birds.

It is all a bunchabloody nonsense, if you get right down to it, and I am not too keen on keeping lists. I do, however, keep a few: a life list, a New Jersey list, a birds seen while hunting list, and a year list.

So let's have a look-see at the old 1995 list. Lists, by the way, are kept in phylogenetic order, starting with the loons and grebes, and ending with the finches.

Loons. Got 'em all, meaning the three realistically possible species for New Jersey: common, red-throated and Pacific. Pacific loon is a rarity, a "goody" if you will, that this year turned up on Spruce Run in Hunterdon County.

Ducks. Got 'em all, including the toughies like the eiders, and the super-tough Barrow's goldeneye.

Shorebirds. Not bad, found most species, including that marvelously colored ruff at Cape May. I missed Hudsonian godwit, though. That bird is a jinx for me.

Gulls and terns. Fine.

Owls, cuckoos, woodpeckers, flycatchers. Great.

Vireos and warblers. Good golly, did I miss mourning warbler!? I never miss that. I'd better check my field notes. Ah, here it is, found a singing male on Point Mountain on June 4.

Sparrows. Nuts, I missed lark sparrow. It's a rare bird, and I never chased any of the ones that were reported on the hot line. There is a tape-recorded birding hot line, updated weekly, that details what birds are being seen around the state. Serious listers call often, and "chase" the birds they are missing. I guess I am not serious enough about this business.

Non-birders by now are thinking that birders are pretty flaky. I don't deny it ... but hang on a minute while I count.

And ladies and gentlemen, the number is... 300 species in New Jersey in 1995. 300 is supposed to be par, but I never quite seem to get there. Perhaps this year I will.

The weather outside

I often wonder what effect approaching or departing weather systems have on the movements of wildlife. I wonder in the context of the fact that, on some days, wildlife can be inconspicuous and difficult to find, despite apparently optimum weather. This type of day seems to coincide too often with days when I am actually out looking.

On other days, there is a hawk in every tree and a fox in every field, so to speak.

Such a day was last Friday, when waves of low-pressure systems moved north along a huge Arctic air mass. Six inches of snow were to fall Friday night over much of the area.

Friday was errand day for me, and while driving to and fro with firewood, broken storm windows and 2-by-4 boards, I saw a variety of wildlife, moving and feeding actively.

A Cooper's hawk pursued rock doves over the farmland across from the elementary school. The American kestrel perched on the wires nearby presumably hunted as well.

Farther north, 15 wild turkeys scratched for insects and acorns in a forest opening not far from the New Jersey State Police barracks. A red-tailed hawk, carrying some sort of prey, soared over the highway near the Hunterdon Medical Center, with four crows in hot pursuit. Several groups of deer fed at midday in the fields and woods along a wooded county road.

The most unusual of the lot was the rough-legged hawk perched right next to the road a couple miles north of my home. This is the exact location where, in 1994, the first rough-legged I ever saw in Hunterdon County passed the winter, making me wonder whether it is the same individual, back from the Arctic.

Rough-leggeds nest inside the Arctic circle during the short northern summer, and are well adapted to the cold. Their legs, for example, are feathered to the toes, hence their name. Rough-leggeds build deep twig nests on cliffs, and line them with moss to insulate the eggs against the tundra winds and cold. This bird probably enjoys our winter weather!

Classically, it is said that wildlife is active and feeds heavily before approaching bad weather. Animals then hole up in their various ways, using den trees, thick conifers and swampy thickets, until the stormy weather passes, moving and feeding again after the skies clear. This explanation, though an over-simplification, often works out in practice.

Many questions remain. How do animals know when a change in the weather is approaching? Many naturalists believe some kinds of wildlife can detect changes in barometric pressure, although there is evidence both pro and con to this belief. Perhaps they just "look outside," only seeing different signs than the TV weatherman. Perhaps a change in wind direction can prompt them to alter their habits. All these theories most likely have at least some truth.

In any case, looking for wildlife a day or so ahead of the next storm will likely be rewarding.

Warm thoughts

The temperature at the shore on Sunday was a not-so-bad 20 degrees Fahrenheit. It was the wind that made trouble that day, howling as it was at 25 to 30 miles per hour and sending the wind chill way below zero.

At the end of the Barnegat Light jetty, stunning harlequin ducks, rare eiders and rarer northern gulls awaited birders prepared to endure the severe conditions. While we watched, several groups of people, well armed with expensive binoculars and spotting scopes, made the trek to the end of the jetty. They would stay for a few moments, but looked so miserable it was clear they would not last long.

I thought, "Those people would have a lot more fun if they knew how to dress to keep warm." Keeping warm is not so difficult, nor is it necessary to buy a whole truckload of winter clothing. Cold weather activities merely require adherence to several key principles.

The basic, overriding principle is to dress in layers that insulate while allowing your body to "breathe." Clothes that breathe allow perspiration to escape, instead of holding it against your skin where the moisture will quickly chill the body. Wearing layered clothing allows for changing conditions: For example, heavy sweaters and coats can be removed when traveling in a car, and put back on when needed to face the elements.

There is a good deal of latitude in what to choose for the outer layers of clothing. Sometimes I pull on one or more wool sweaters, other times a jacket made of a synthetic material like Polarfleece. For the legs, I normally wear loose-fitting jeans over a good set of long johns. In severe cold, I top my outfit off with a heavy parka. A parka insulated with Thinsulate and covered with a breathable, wind-breaking coating like Gore-tex is ideal, but a less high-tech coat will work fine if you wear several layers beneath. I am certain most people can find adequate outer layers already in their closets and drawers.

What a birder or other outdoors person wears against the skin may be the most important garment in the whole outfit. The rule here is that the undergarments must be snug but not tight, and must be made of a moisture-wicking material like polypropylene, Thermax, or another similar material. Cotton is a poor choice for the layer next to the skin, because it absorbs sweat and then holds it chillingly against the skin.

Unfortunately, the long johns carried in department stores are often cotton, and lots of people make the mistake of wearing cotton T-shirts for the first layer.

Everyone knows a warm hat, like a wool watch cap, is very important for keeping warm, as is a scarf or neck gaiter.

But what do you do about feet? Cold feet are a real problem for many people, myself included. I wear heavy wool socks under heavily insulated pac-type boots, and make sure my legs are well insulated but are not garbed so tightly that circulation is impaired.

A final tip: If you know you will be out in the cold, let your healthy diet go for a day and eat hearty, especially high-fat foods like bacon, eggs, or cream cheese. Fat carries the calories necessary for your body to heat itself, is better in the cold than proteins, sugars or starches, and is much better than no food at all.

Into the woods

The winter woods wait quietly, seemingly devoid of animals, so the naturalist turns to things that are always available for study. Like trees, for example.

Until studied closely, in wintertime it seems like a tree is a tree is a tree. Many winter trees can be easily recognized, however, by the texture of their bark, the shape and size of their buds, and even by the overall shape of the tree itself.

Most people recognize a weeping willow's droopy form immediately. Other winter tree-shapes are equally distinctive, once you get to know them.

American elms display a beautiful vase-like shape, with branches arching up and out about halfway up the tree, and ending in delicate pendulous branches at the tip. William Harlow, author of my favorite tree book, writes that the shape of the American elm " ... has been referred to as that of a wineglass, a feather duster, and even a colonial lady upside down."

At any rate, it is a beautiful tree. Open-grown white oaks show a characteristic round shape, with large branches spreading in all directions around the trunk. Lateral branches in white oaks can be quite long, because the oak's strong wood can support heavy limbs reaching for the sun. I often see these big oaks along fencerows in farm country. Many big trees are found along hedgerows, stone walls and streams, where as seedlings they were safe from the farmer's mower and his grazing cows.

Hikers along rivers, or near other wet areas, will often find stands of trees with many dead branches hanging down on the lower part of the trunks. These are pin oaks, an abundant wetland tree. Pin oak was so-named because the wood was used to make pins for holding together the beams and timbers for barns. Maybe the name is also from the acorns, which are quite small, although not so small as the head of a pin.

Now is the time to tap maple trees for their sap, so it would be nice if winter maples were as easy to identify as some other winter trees. They are not. Sugar maple bark, and tree shape, are pretty variable. The branches of maples are opposite, meaning that each branch has an opposing one on the opposite side of the limb, unless one is broken off. Ashes and dogwoods also have opposite branching, however.

Sugar maples do have distinctive fruit: the two-winged "helicopters" that kids love to toss in the air. Perhaps it would be better to identify which trees to tap in autumn, when the leaves are still around.

Maple sugaring, by the way, is about as American an activity as there is, because, courtesy of the American Indians, this country is the birthplace of syruping. Harlow writes that "to taste the cold sweet sap as it drips from the tree is part of every American's birthright!"

The sap is flowing in the trees, spring can't be far behind, and soon we'll have leaves to help us identify the trees again.

Masked marvel

A raccoon wandered fat and sassy across my backyard shortly before dark the other night. I called the kids to the window to see it, but the raccoon heard my voice from outside and waddled into the thicket fringing our yard before they got to the window. This was probably just as well, because our dog, Rachel, bounded right behind the kids, and Rachel goes nuts when she sees even a chipmunk outside.

I wondered why that raccoon rushed nightfall. Usually raccoons wait for dark before moving around. This one was obviously healthy and alert, so disease was not responsible. Perhaps it was a male starting the late winter breeding season, or one that knew of a particularly good spot to find food and was hurrying to get there before other raccoons.

Seeing a raccoon always makes me happy, and I have not been seeing too many since the recent wave of rabies and distemper washed over the Northeast. The wave receded, however, and raccoons seem to be making a comeback. This is good news to me, although I am sure sanitation workers and farmers feel differently.

The raccoon is one of those animals, like the white-tailed deer or gray squirrel, that adapts remarkably well to man's occupancy of the planet. Raccoons would just as soon eat leftover chicken as crayfish, and effectively use storm sewers as highways from one garbage can to the next.

A friend at the New Jersey Division of Fish, Game and Wildlife told me about a graduate student who used radio telemetry to study raccoon movements in a suburban area. He would drive slowly down development streets late at night, antenna hanging out the window of his car, waiting for a signal from one of his transmitter-equipped raccoons. The student would then park near a storm drain, and watch as first a nose and then the masked face of the furry bandit emerged from the drain. The raccoon would look all around, checking to see if the coast was clear, and then waddle for the nearest garbage can.

Raccoons are capable of doing substantial damage to farm crops, especially corn. Be it sweet or field corn, raccoons will stuff themselves full of it, often wasting a bunch in the process. Usually a raccoon will leave quite a bit of corn on an ear, preferring to rip down a fresh one after only a few bites. I think raccoon damage in farm fields is often blamed on deer.

Be that as it may, I would rather have raccoons around than not. They are attractive enough, with a thick fur coat and mischievous black mask, and seem as inquisitive as children at times.

The Algonquins called raccoons "arakunem," which means "he who scratches with his hands." Raccoons like to handle things, and in fact come as close as any North American animal (excepting humans) to having hands instead of paws.

I remember one early morning when I sat near a downed tree and watched a family of raccoons, mother and three little ones, walk along the trunk only an arm's length away. Mom didn't trust the funny-looking lump dressed in camouflage and scurried across, but the little ones paused and stared eagerly, occasionally reaching out with their paws as if eager to try the binoculars dangling from my neck.

I would have let them take a look, but I was afraid they'd make off with the things.

Chickadee warmth

One very cold day not too long ago, I returned from a walk to find our feeder alive with birds. One chickadee scolded cheerfully as I shivered up to the door; another perched puffed round as a golf ball on a sunlit branch not three feet away.

My teeth stopped chattering to grin, and a thought struck me. How can they stand it? How in the world can something that small, a hundred times lighter than the clothes I was wearing, thrive in cold that daunted me after only an hour?

Thanks to the work of other ecologists, finding the answer in the library was simple, but the knowing made the fact of it no less miraculous.

Birds, on the average, maintain a body temperature 3 to 4 degrees higher than a typical mammal. Small birds like chickadees must keep their body temperatures at 107 degrees Fahrenheit. They possess several physiological and behavioral adaptations to accomplish this.

As anyone with a down jacket knows, feathers insulate remarkably well. This is because of the air spaces between them. Chickadees wear about 2,000 body feathers, and control their positions very precisely. A chickadee puffs up its feathers to increase the air spaces insulating its body from the outside temperature.

Birds are built well to resist the cold. Most of their muscle mass is held close to the body, reducing the loss of heat through extremities such as legs and arms that plagues humans. Bird legs are essentially bone and ligament; their feet are moved much as we might move a puppet, via connecting ligaments and tendons.

Many animals, including birds, have a remarkable circulatory adaptation to reduce heat loss through extremities. This adaptation is the alignment of arterial and venous blood vessels, where they flow through the extremities. Arteries carrying warm blood from inside the body transfer heat back to returning venous blood. This alignment allows the extremities to be much colder than normal body temperature, but maintains the much more important core temperature.

Chickadees frequently rest in the winter sun with their feathers puffed out, soaking up solar energy. They and many other winter birds roost in tree cavities at night to conserve heat.

As a last resort, birds like chickadees can increase their metabolic rate to increase heat production. This is a last resort because, just like increasing the setting on your home thermostat, increasing metabolic rate requires more fuel. During severe cold, birds must eat more and better food. At feeding stations, foods with high fat content, such as suet or sunflower seeds, receive the most attention from cold weather visitors.

After my walk, I thawed next to the fireplace, glad for its warmth, and equally glad for the chickadee warmth outside.

Special moments

Sometimes it seems to me that a huge amount of time spent looking at the natural world compresses itself into a few relatively tiny moments, small vignettes of insight into the lives of the creatures that share the land with us. These vignettes are the scenes you see on the TV nature shows, a few frames of fascinating images clipped from hours of quiet footage. Remarkably, twice last weekend I experienced scenes TV cameramen seldom can film.

The first happened as I stood scanning for waterfowl on the chilly shore of Columbia Lake. Thin ice lined the lake edge, and after a few minutes of scanning I heard the occasional crackling of something small breaking the ice.

A scan to the north revealed a sinewy brown something slipping along the shore toward me. Occasionally, the ice broke beneath it, and it swam in the chilly water for a few feet until it could climb out again.

Rich brown fur, medium-long tail, white chin, pink nose, weasel-like; the animal closed to 20 feet before I realized with a start I was watching a wild mink, an animal I have seen only once before, and not nearly so well.

Fifteen feet away, the mink paused on a downed tree, rubbing its face on the wood and stretching luxuriously. There he (or she) stayed for a minute or more, oblivious to my presence until the wind shifted and blew my scent up the shoreline. Immediately the mink stood up on its hindquarters, glanced nervously about, and scampered back up the shore the way it had come.

From a naturalist's viewpoint, the weekend was complete, and it was only Saturday! But another film-quality sighting enlivened Sunday, too.

This time, Dave Womer of Bloomsbury and I were birding together, counting bird species and individuals for the Northwest Hunterdon Christmas Bird Count. I had been "pishing," which means imitating bird alarm calls in an attempt to draw birds into view. As part of pishing, I usually do a few screech owl calls, and despite the fact that it was mid-day, I shortly heard an owl responding to the calls.

Pinpointing the owl was difficult, because as I walked a few steps up and down the road the source of the calls seemed to shift dramatically, as if the bird were flying back and fourth. After a while longer than it should have taken, I realized the owl called from the cherry tree right next to me, and circling to the other side of the tree I saw a likely cavity reachable with a little climbing.

Dave came over and boosted me to the tree's first limb, and soon I peered down into the hole – and right into the face of a screech owl!

The distance

A series of dark specks pass across the scope's field of view, disappearing and reappearing behind five-foot swells. All dark. Are you sure? Yes. No white in the wings? No. No white on the heads? No. Can you really tell from here? Probably not. Black scoters. How do you know? Because.

The 17 specks round the jetty at Island Beach and swing away from the wind, suddenly gaining 20 knots worth of speed as they enter the bay. You know the weather's bad when scoters start looking for shelter.

Back to the scope. One hand steadies from above, the other twists the focus, which is stiff from the cold. The hand is stiff, too. There is only so much nylon, Gore-tex, and Thinsulate can do.

Distant ducks bob and dive on the swells, mostly skinny-necked-dark-and-whites (mergansers), with a smattering of fat-dark-and-whites (bufflehead) and a lonely brown smudge (female eider) that has eluded close scrutiny (and identification to species) by diving every time a gap in the waves opens her to view. This in accordance with Freiday's Theorem on Diving Birds, which states:

The speed and timing of a bird's dive are directly related to the speed and timing of the closest birder. The bird will dive 0.1 seconds before the binoculars reach the eyes, or 0.01 seconds after the bird is found in a spotting scope.

There are two corollaries to Freiday's Theorem, one of which concerns warblers and is irrelevant here. The other states:

A diving bird, after diving, will never re-surface while in a spotting scope's field of view.

Everything is far away, so you are birding the distance. Which is good. Most of what you look at in winter are ducks, and real birders know that ducks are easy to identify. Ducks are big and slow and have bright patterns, so distance and bad weather makes the birding more, how shall we say, sporting. (No one looks at female, immature, or eclipse-plumaged ducks.)

Seriously, searching out into the distance in winter is wonderfully heuristic. Why, you might ask, do ducks dive actively some of the time and sit still some of the time? The answer bobs with the rise and fall of the tide. If a scoter scrapes mollusks from the bottom of the jetty, it makes sense for the bird to wait until low tide to feed, because then it doesn't have so far to dive for dinner.

How, you might ask, can these birds survive immersed in ice water in the first place? I mean, they actually look comfortable out there. The ducks coat their feathers with oil from their preen gland, and everyone knows what eider down is famous for. Scoter down does the same thing. Birds also have a useful countercurrent circulation system in their legs, where outgoing arterial blood warms cooled, incoming venous blood. High metabolism and plenty to eat also help the ducks keep warm.

Why, you might ask in a fit of reflection, did the Labrador duck go extinct? No one really knows, but if it still shared our world, it might be a hoped-for rarity off our coast in winter. The bird was apparently most closely related to the eiders. The last Labrador duck specimen was shot in 1875, but like most sea ducks the species was not favored for eating, and so commercial hunting alone would not cause its demise. No one is even sure where Labrador ducks nested.

Who, you might ask in pain, was the liar who said these boots were good to minus-50 degrees Fahrenheit? Sorry, no boots will keep your feet warm if your legs, torso and head aren't warm, too. Wear silk or polypropylene long underwear, loose but warm pants, a down or Thinsulate vest, a coat that will break the wind, a heavy wool watch cap, a scarf, and most of all remember: Cold is good.

Where, you might ask, are all these rare birds I am supposed to be seeing? The guide book calls black-legged kittewakes "fairly common winter visitors" around here. Can you give that to me in terms of how many hours I have to stand here until I see one, please?

What, you might ask, what on God's green earth would possess me to stand out here like this? Way, way out there, out beyond the breakers, beyond the ducks, is where to look for the answer to that one. For what? A gannet, an alcid, a skua? A boat full of elves, an angel, a mermaid? You find out. Look way out there. If you can stand it. For there are a number of heretofore unmentioned prerequisites for seeing the distance.

You must be alone. I know, I know, birding is supposed to be a fraternal – paternal? maternal? infernal? – activity, where friends or family gather to enjoy the wonders of nature (or perhaps a bit of spirited competition).

Bunk. You have to be alone. The weather has to be good for birding, which means a nor'easter or plain 'easter, and vicious, numbing, searing cold. Cold and wind to make your eyes tear as you look offshore, your scope shaking, your fingers stiff, your metal tripod painful to the touch.

Consider it a sacred ritual, like the sun rituals of the Plains Indians.

You have to patient. Remember, this isn't TV. This is nature au natural. Reality. You might see something alive every scan. You might see something alive every hour. You might not see anything new, but you will see something.

If you see a goodie way out there, meaning a rare bird, and your first thought is "Hah! I can't wait to tell so-and-so" or "Hah! Only an expert could have picked that one out," go home. You're not doing it right. Besides, so-and-so isn't going to believe you.

Sometimes the most distant thing I find while standing out on a jetty is inside, anyway.

Some people don't even want to see into distance. Some people don't want to endure discomfort. If those people are reading this ... well, I don't understand you, either.

As the crow flies

The sound of crows raising a ruckus usually is worth investigating. If they give shrieking caws, like fans at a hockey game, they are almost always hassling a great-horned owl. Something about these big owls excites the lust for blood in crows.

The flocks of black birds treat each owl they discover like a mortal enemy, which is puzzling considering the owl's diet. A great-horned pretty much sticks to animals with fur on them when it looks for a meal.

I doubt an owl eats crow very much.

If a milling flock of crows sounds less enthused, perhaps like the gallery watching a golf tournament, they probably are busy ruining a red-tailed hawk's day. It is common to see a redtail and one or two crows "dog-fighting" over fields or dodging each other through forests.

Red-tailed are powerful birds, and people often wonder why they don't put a speedy end to their tormentors. The reason is the alacrity with which a crow can elude the red-tailed's swiftest attack. Red-taileds are built to soar and drop suddenly on unsuspecting small mammals, not to engage in acrobatics with a bird half their weight. Crows can make a fool out of any red-tailed hawk that flies, and plenty of other birds besides. Crows are supposed to be one of our most intelligent birds, and generally choose their battles wisely. In fact, I can only recall one time when I watched a crow receive its comeuppance.

This happened many years ago at Liberty State Park in Jersey City. Liberty Park at that time was a prime spot to find short-eared owls, which are crow-sized and crow-quick, and seem to have a fairly short fuse.

On this occasion, a short-eared owl flushed from tall salt-marsh grass on the mainland, well away from any other suitable cover for these ground-roosting birds. The owl took off for, of all places, the Statue of Liberty. Maybe it was going to perch on the torch? The statue towered over Newark Bay at least a mile away, forcing the bird to fly a long way over open water.

Anyway, a crow spotted the vulnerable owl almost immediately and began to dive on it. Watching the short-eared dip and dive to avoid the onslaught, I was feeling pretty guilty for flushing it and causing it all this trouble, and unconsciously started rooting for the owl.

Things looked grim for the owl. Each pass by the crow forced the short-eared closer to the water, and several times the crow actually struck the owl on the back. But I could almost see the owl's frustration turning into anger; I could almost see that fuse burning down.

The short-eared owl was nearly swimming when he made his move. The crow confidently dove on him, but this time met nothing but sharp talons as the short-eared barrel-rolled and grabbed the crow in claws normally reserved for meadow voles. The owl completed his roll with the crow still in his clutches, then calmly dropped the bird into Newark Bay, and flew on toward the statue. The crow, meanwhile, flapped its way out of the water and struggled soggily towards shore.

I guess that time the crow ate crow.

Opossums

While walking along a small tributary to the Neshanic River during last weekend's thaw, I discovered some opossum tracks in the melting snow. The melting and freezing snow had altered the tracks somewhat. The track outlines were obscure, and the tracks appeared twice as large as normal opossum tracks.

This phenomenon of tracks increasing in size in snow that has alternated between melting and freezing sometimes leads to embarrassing errors. Distorted dog tracks have been identified as bear tracks, and bear or human tracks altered this way probably gave rise to the legend of that hairy creature of the Northwest, Bigfoot.

The size of these opossum tracks puzzled me as to their maker, until I noticed that some of the tracks showed an inner toe pointing away from the rest of the foot. Since opossums are the only local mammal with an opposable inner toe, the odd toe's presence clinched the identification.

Opossums are unique animals. The species is the only marsupial found in North America, and is one of the most primitive mammals still existing today. Paleontologists have found bones from opossums in deposits formed during the Cretaceous period, back when the dinosaurs were enjoying their heyday. You cannot argue with the design of an animal that has survived 100 million years. By comparison, modern humans evolved something like 2 million years ago.

How did opossums last so long? It certainly was not brain power. If you ever have a chance to examine an opossum skull, notice the size of the brain case. A Hershey kiss would just about fit inside. Opossums are not too bright, but extreme intelligence is not necessary for their lifestyle. After all, they do not need to surf the Internet, or even file income-tax reports.

While you are examining your opossum skull, notice the teeth. There are 50, more teeth than any North American mammal. Opossums survive by being adaptable, especially about what they eat. They go forth each night to search for food, and food includes just about anything, including putrid meat, frogs, small mammals, acorns, grapes, insects ... you name it. In fact, an opossum hungry for grilled game hen precipitated one of the first arguments my wife, Cathy, and I ever had as a married couple.

We were on our honeymoon, preparing dinner at a campground in Cape May. Two Cornish game hens roasted over the crackling fire, and we were happily basking in the firelight when the proprietor of the campground came to say we had a telephone call (I have since dispensed with campgrounds for camping, whenever there is a more isolated alternative.)

When we returned to the fire, America's most primitive mammal was standing next to it, chewing greedily on our game hens! It hissed and bared its teeth at our approach.

Responding with equally primitive instincts, I groped about in the dark for something with which to club that 'possum. My arm was back to strike when Cathy said, "Don't you dare."

I didn't, and the opossum waddled off, happily dragging away our dinner.

Frogs

"Bud. Bud. Bud."

"Weis." "Bud." "Weis." "Bud." "Weis." "Er." "Bud." "Weis." "Er."

Final score to the contrary, 1995's Super Bowl was not a total waste of time: The Budweiser frog commercial had at least one fan rolling on the carpet. Perhaps ABC Television should pay the advertisers a million dollars a minute for programming, instead of the other way around.

Bud frogs are probably sitting on the lily pads of the future, entertaining the genetic engineers who developed this ultimate Madison Avenue scheme. Imagine: a fleet of frogs hopping across the U.S., calling the name of your client's product. The managers at Coors are shaking in their hip boots, or maybe they are trying to slightly alter the COOing of doves. The folks who pushed for a biotechnology department when I was at Rutgers were right; there really is money to be made in genetic engineering.

I digress. It will be two or three months before frogs will be "Budweisering" around here. Spring peepers hop to water's edge in mid-March for their peepfest, followed by quacking wood frogs a few weeks later. Green frogs wait until May brings warmer waters before they squirm from the mucky pond bottoms. A real green frog call was audible in the original Budweiser commercial, by the way, though the Bud's and er's nearly drowned out its "guunnng."

Two commonly asked questions about hibernating frogs:

1) How do they breathe when they are down in the mud, and

2) How do they know when to come out?

The breathing question is a complicated one. Frogs hibernating at the bottom of ponds or swamps have dramatically reduced metabolisms, because all life processes are slowed in the near-freezing temperatures of a body of water in winter. The limited oxygen needed at this low level of activity can be obtained through extrapulmonary gas exchange – a fancy way of saying breathing

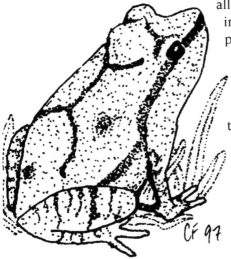

CF 97

through the skin.

Under some circumstances, hibernating frogs probably need no oxygen at all; the minimal amount of metabolic activity required can be accomplished using anaerobic respiration, which is exactly what happens when a weight-lifter performs an exercise. Lactic acid builds up in the body during anaerobic activity, but apparently not enough to be harmful to the dormant frogs.

Frogs use one of three cues to decide when to become active in the spring. Like just about all forms of wildlife, frogs respond to changes in day length. A frog hibernating in the mud might have a difficult time knowing when the sun is rising and setting, however.

A better sign of spring for frogs is water temperature, and this signal is probably the most important one to frogs. Warm, rainy nights in spring often prompt the emergence of frogs, or yield an increase in activity levels or calling.

Frogs also may have some sort of internal clock, which is set before hibernation by the length of daylight in the fall and goes off when the time to emerge rolls around. The internal clock may be in the form of a chemical that builds up to a specific level in the frog's body by emergence time, or one that is used up by that time.

A fourth possible cue is the fireworks of the Superbowl halftime show, but I doubt anyone will go mucking around outside next year to check this hypothesis.

Sleepers

Quite a few misconceptions seem to be floating around about what wild animals do in the winter. The most popular theme is hibernation. Hibernation has been ascribed to everything with fur and four legs on it, but the truth is that only four kinds of mammals in our area totally conk out until spring. Bats, bears, chipmunks and ground hogs are the sleepers although some bats migrate before – or instead of – hibernating. All the other mammals are active most of the time all season.

Now, as soon as I say that bears hibernate, someone's going to get technical with me and say that since a bear's body temperature doesn't drop significantly, they are not really hibernators. The fact is, if something spends the entire winter in a den without moving, it hibernates. A bear's core temperature does not drop, because the bear would consume too many precious calories to heat back up again.

Chipmunks and bats are little, so it does not take a lot of time or fuel for them to heat up once they have cooled down. In fact, chipmunks often "wake up" during winter warm spells, or even cold spells, and feed on some of the food they have stored for the winter.

Ground hogs are bigger, and have a harder time getting from the 37-degree body temperature they hibernate at to their normal 96 degrees.

In most years, ground hogs don't wake up on purpose at all until March, which means that the jokers who wake up poor Poxawhoosit Joe (or whatever his name is) for the reporters on Feb. 2 aren't doing the animal any favors.

Now, if a ground hog has a hard time warming up, imagine how long it would take for a 400-pound black bear. If one cooled down for the winter, a bear would burn every ounce of fat he had to warm up again.

By the way, only one species of bird is known to hibernate. The common poorwill, a bird of the western United States, has occasionally been found to remain in a torpid condition for extended periods of time.

It should be pointed out that just because an animal is active all winter, it does not mean it is active at all times all winter. Opossums, raccoons, squirrels, rabbits and skunks, for example, will den for several days if the weather turns especially nasty. Even foxes, weasels and deer will lay in a sheltered location to ride out a storm. Animals seem to have more sense than people when it comes to staying home when the weather is bad. At any rate, all these species will resume activity when the storm or Arctic cold dissipates.

Deer have an interesting strategy for the winter. Like all wild creatures, they feed very heavily in the fall, in an effort to put on layers of fat for the hard times ahead. When winter finally rolls around, deer enter a sort of "walking hibernation," in which bodily functions and daily activities are reduced to conserve energy.

I am sure you know people like this.

Oh, deer!

One of my earliest memories, drawn from my late-1960s toddler-hood, is of my father calling us all to the window with the cry, "Deer in the clearing!"

We would rush to the nearest window or door, and (in my case) stare with mixed awe and wonder as the sleek, graceful creatures eased carefully across the 3-acre meadow behind our home. They never lingered, never stayed in full view for long. My father used to tell the story of the time in his boyhood when, after a doe appeared near a hedgerow on their farm, his mother called the neighbors and excitedly described where it was and which way it was headed.

Times have changed, so have people, and something dramatic and (in my view) wonderful has happened to the white-tailed deer. Actually, three things have happened, more or less at the same time. By the early 1980s, the deer population had increased to its current high level over much of the Northeast. Meanwhile, the amount of deer habitat decreased dramatically due to development, especially in the past 20 years. Finally, the deer themselves have become a lot more tolerant of human disturbance, in effect re-defining "habitat" to include suburban lawns and roadsides.

More deer are thus more visible to more people, and deer-people encounters, good and bad, happen so frequently that they pass without mention anymore.

The white-tailed deer is very likely the second-most studied animal on earth (after homo sapiens), a fact indicative of its popularity, at least with the wildlife management sect.

"White-tailed Deer: Ecology and Management," the everything-you-ever-wanted-to-know-about-deer book and a beautiful one at that, is 870 pages of small print long and lists more than 2,200 references in its bibliography. So there certainly is no shortage of information on deer.

Deer are popular with non-managers, too, and with good cause. No one who watches a whitetail bound effortlessly through a woodland, cleanly jump a 7-foot fence, or race across a meadow, can dispute the deer's physical appeal. For me, deer lend a sense of wildness to any scene; if they were removed from the woods, the woods would suffer.

If only they would stay in the woods!

A suburban resident, disgruntled but amused by the "hoofed locusts" plaguing his several thousands dollars worth of landscape shrubs, theorized to me once that archaeologists excavating the remains of the town thousands of years from now might think they had discovered an extremely anti-social community. What else would explain the 8-foot-high chain-link fencing surrounding each dwelling? Another garden lover, considerably less tolerant, suggested the use of land mines to control the herd.

Much of the garden and landscape damage problem is the fault of modern horticulture. We plant species selected for their appearance and with no regard to their palatability. Then we fertilize and water them to make them the most succulent growth around. Studies have shown that, when given a choice, deer will choose fertilized plants over unfertilized ones every time. Deer, as ruminants, are wonderfully adapted to the depredation of gardens and landscape shrubs. They are able to eat very hastily, filling their rumens in just a few hours, and then retire to a safe area to chew their cud. Thus, they visit lawns and gardens under the cover of darkness, leaving before dawn to digest their meal in the safety of a nearby woodlot or overgrown field. Only, these days they often don't bother with waiting for the cover of darkness.

Deer adapt marvelously well to humans – and human behavior. They know very well the difference between the mailman, the children waiting for the bus, and someone stalking them intending to do harm. They can be incredibly brazen when they conclude that an encounter will not end with a bullet.

Deer cause much greater problems, of course, than nipping off the freshly planted impatiens. About 10,000 are hit by cars every year in my home state of New Jersey, causing millions of dollars worth of property damage, and once in a while a human fatality.

They have also been fingered, perhaps unjustly, as the chief life-support mechanism of the adult deer tick, the vector of Lyme disease.

It is hard to imagine that a deer population comparable to today's could be reduced to almost zero, but in New Jersey's case, by 1900 the wild deer herd was reduced to a few family groups eking out an existence in the Pine Barrens. This was in spite of the fact that the colonists' lumbering, burning and agricultural activities improved habitat for the edge-loving deer. The deer disappeared because they were over-exploited by the settlers, and especially by the once thrifty American Indians, who began trading deer hides and hams for guns, goods and liquor.

There is some question as to how abundant deer were in pre-Columbian times, which is unfortunate because it would be very interesting to know the whitetail's true abundance before white men came along. There are theories and calculations and a few estimations by long-ago naturalists, most of which indicate that deer were not more or less common than they are now.

For a long time biologists believed that white-tailed deer were generally less common in pre-colonial times than they are today. This theory was founded on the belief, now questioned, that pre-Columbian eastern North America was one vast, mature forest, providing far less than optimum conditions for the edge-loving deer. Deer in this scenario would be confined mostly to river banks, coastal wetlands, and other infrequent openings in the forest.

In reality, the pre-Columbian forest probably had many

breaks and clearings, created by wildfires and especially by fires intentionally set by native Americans. The American Indian, long held up as a paradigm of environmental awareness, no doubt knew that deer preferred forest openings for foraging. Indians also cleared land for agriculture.

One way of estimating pre-colonial deer abundance is to derive population figures from numbers of deer killed, or presumed to have been killed, by Indians and early settlers. Some hunts in the Great Lakes Region, for example, accounted for a minimum of 50 deer per square mile, a figure matched in New Jersey only in the higher deer-density areas. Estimates of the number of deer killed by each Indian hunter for food, clothing and implements vary, with a range of estimates between five and 150 annually. Most estimates fall in the range of 10-20. If 7,000 Indians lived in New Jersey when the first settlers arrived (a moderate estimate), and one in every five hunted, and each hunter killed 15 deer per year (also a moderate estimate), then 21,000 deer per year were being taken. Since a healthy deer herd increases by 30 to 40 percent per year, a minimum of 65,000 deer must have been present in the state for the population to remain stable. This figure is reached without allowing for deer killed by non-human predators, which in New Jersey, before white men arrived, included wolves and eastern cougars.

(A digression: What about non-human predators? I frequently hear people, including some respected naturalists, saying that the reason we have so many deer in New Jersey now is because we have eliminated all their "natural" predators, meaning chiefly wolves but also eastern cougars, bobcats and bears. This may not be true. Under most conditions, wolves and other predators do not seem to be able on their own to limit a deer population. Maximum wolf densities are usually on the order of one per 10 square miles. To sustain this wolf density, even if wolves ate only deer, which they don't, the deer population needs to be only about three per square mile, which is way, way less than it is over good whitetail range now. It is unfortunate that the exact historic densities of deer and their predators are not known, but deer herds historically probably were not "controlled" by predators except under unusual circumstances. Deer abundance and availability probably had much greater influence on predator abundance than the other way around. End of digression.)

At any rate, the deer were about gone by 1900, despite anti-exploitation strictures beginning with a 1679 act prohibiting the export of hides from Indian-killed deer and ending with complete abolishment of hunting on a county- or statewide basis by the late 1800's. Whitetails were re- established with a series of stocking efforts between 1904 and 1920; sportsmen and the forerunner of the modern Fish and Game Council initiated these stockings. Approximately two hundred deer were obtained from Michigan, Pennsylvania, and from several private, fenced preserves within the New Jersey and released. Fallow deer, released at the same time in a introduction effort, fortunately did not survive. Under strict and ever-more-sophisticated hunting regulations, the herd increased through the early 1980s to the 150,000-160,000 range.

For better or worse, depending on one's point of view on deer hunting, the New Jersey deer herd has been stabilized at this level for the past 10 years by hunting (50,000, plus or minus, are shot annually) and car collisions (estimated at 10,000 annually). The state Division of Fish, Game and Wildlife calls the current population level the "cultural carrying capacity," meaning that the state's habitat could support more deer but the state's people could not put up with them.

I am puzzled sometimes by people who become annoyed at the white-tailed deer. Shouldn't we be glad that at least one species seems able to adapt to the changes wrought by our own? Aren't we especially lucky that that species also happens to be big, beautiful and graceful? I for one wish worm-eating warblers and bobcats and barred owls coped as well as white-tails. And, although it happens almost every day, I still call out to my family when there is a deer out back.

Signs of spring

I found the subjects of this essay in the back yard this morning. They stood on the snow honking and grimacing at the ice still on the pond and the snow still covering the grass.

They could not have come at a better time. I visited friends in Cape May over the weekend, and became highly jealous because although the grass is still brown down there, at least it is visible. I recommend a trip to Cape May, by the way, to overcome the standard space-time continuum problems that ordinarily force people to go to Florida or the Bahamas to hurry spring along. It's like a different country down there. For example, red-winged blackbirds have arrived in force and are already singing their "conk-ka-rees" from the tops of reeds in the wetlands along the Delaware Bay shore. Hunterdon County and parts north have not even seen the first red-wing of spring!

Anyway, I woke up this morning to find a pair of Canada geese standing on the icy back yard, gazing at the island in the pond that they are hoping to nest on in a few weeks.

This is the same island where they nested last year. I have no doubt whatsoever that it's the same pair; they knew what they were about when they landed. The male, identifiable because of his slightly larger size, honked occasionally, while after a short inspection the female settled her bottom down on the ice.

It was apparent that the geese were there with the intent of re-establishing their breeding territory. A pair of Canadas will return to the same traditional nesting area year after year, defending it against would-be interlopers. By arriving at their chosen site so early in the year (far too early, cold and icy to actually nest), this pair was gaining an advantage in defending the site from later birds. The phrase, "possession is nine-tenths of ownership" was never better applied than to geese on a farm pond.

Geese are unusual among birds in that family groups tend to stay together most of the year. If these two birds were just on their regular winter rounds, chances are they would be with their young from last year or the year before. Geese take two to three years to reach maturity, which explains why flocks of non-breeders are often present locally during the breeding season. Family groups break up just before the onset of nesting.

I wish I could offer another sign of spring to cheer you up, but it looks like winter has a pretty good grip at the moment. I came upon a fox sparrow the other day, but I am sure he is wintering locally, rather than being an early migrant. I did hear a cardinal singing merrily one sunny morning in Bloomsbury, although 10 below zero hardly feels like spring on the door step.

Many birds of prey have flown to greener pastures. I have been unable to locate either short-eared owls or long-eared owls for the first winter in many years. These birds eat mice and voles almost exclusively, and the icy-snow covering keeps the rodents safe and the owls hungry.

Oh well. In just a few weeks we'll have our own red- winged blackbirds, and then spring peepers peeping and skunk cabbage poking up through the mud, and spring will be here again.

Spring

Eastern phoebe

Spring

Woodcock comes a'courting

If near your home lies a wettish sort of field or meadow next to a wettish sort of woods (what other sorts of fields and woods are there in March?), you might be interested in going out some evening shortly after sundown to listen for a small bird with a long bill and a rather extravagant way of hooking up with lady friends.

What do you listen for? Well, the first note of this bird, which is called the American woodcock, sounds something like the word "peent" spoken while holding one's nose. Go ahead, try it ... I'll wait.

The woodcock begins his "peenting" at about 6:30 p.m. at this time of year. "Peenting" is just a warm-up for the full-blown nuptial display that follows. While he "peents," the male woodcock struts back and forth on the edge of the field. Since dusk is already thick, this part of the display is difficult to observe. If this behavior could be seen, the observer would see a robin-sized, plumply built shorebird with a bill a good 2 inches long.

Although in the shorebird family, the woodcock forsakes the sand and salt marshes, preferring instead dense alder thickets and other swampy areas. The long bill, which houses an even longer tongue, probes moist earth for worms and occasionally other tasty invertebrates.

After "peenting" a few times, the woodcock takes to the air and flies up, up, up in a spectacular spiraling flight that carries him several hundred feet overhead. The bird's wings give a pronounced "whirr" or twitter, and often the sound draws a keen eye to the silhouette of the bird against the sunset.

Next comes the best part: After gaining all the altitude he is going to, the woodcock begins to drop, swerving and accelerating towards the earth, much like a leaf falling in autumn, all the while issuing a remarkable series of notes which run into a song I just cannot describe, so I will not even try. The woodcock alights in the spot he launched from, and summarily begins his "peenting" again until he is ready for another flight.

The object of all this effort on the part of the male woodcock is to attract the attention and gain the favor of a female woodcock. If a female appears on the scene, the male will strut stiff-legged toward her, hoping for a chance to mate.

Woodcock are promiscuous. They do not form a pair bond and the male is not at all involved in incubating the eggs or caring for the young, which probably explains his ability to expend so much effort in courtship.

Lightning

Succumbing to a little spring fever last Sunday, my family and I decided to take a short road trip. We had a fine day, hiking in the wilderness area of the Great Swamp National Wildlife Refuge.

The swamp and environs are my old stomping grounds (I used to call it my natural habitat), and I made sure I picked a remote access point for the hike. On nice Sundays, nature enthusiasts pack the swamp, and although it is a good thing that so many people are interested in nature, the crowds sort of defeat the purpose of wilderness.

The kids ran excitedly looking for their boots before we left, because I let on that they'd be getting their feet wet. Nothing like a little water to discourage other hikers.

Sure enough, not a single car lurked in the gravel parking area. A great blue heron, in lovely breeding plumage, posed in the marsh near the trail's entrance.

The kids found about a zillion interesting things while splashing about; the best thing about kids is that everything can be interesting to them! There was no question, however, as to which was their favorite discovery.

Far back in the swamp we found a huge old tulip tree that lightning had struck, perhaps during a violent electrical storm last summer. The tree, although still standing quite solidly, had absolutely no bark on it. We found some of it, lying scorched several yards away.

It was easy to see why lightning hit the tulip because it was the tallest tree in the vicinity. Interestingly, five or 10 smaller trees in the vicinity apparently got their own dose of electricity, which left their exteriors charred.

Studies with high-speed cameras reveal that most lightning flashes consist of multiple strokes, each of which is preceded by a "leader" stroke. Perhaps the "leader" stroke hit the big tulip, while the subsidiary strokes killed the smaller trees.

That storm must have been awesome to behold; still, I am quite happy to have missed it. In the United States, about 100 people are killed and many more injured by lightning each year, more than by tornadoes or hurricanes.

Lightning is not all bad, however. Nitrogen released from the atmosphere by lightning enriches the soil when carried to the ground by raindrops. Some scientists believe that lightning may have been a key element in the origin of life on earth. It is thought that the energy from lightning created large molecules from simple elements, and that these complex chemicals gave rise to living matter.

My sons, Timmy and Donny, found another use for lightning. When I suggested that the Native Americans Indians probably smeared charred wood on their faces to camouflage themselves, the two rubbed their hands on the bark and then on their faces.

Peepers

Spring called on March 15, debuting with a front of luke-warm squalls. The signals were mixed at first, though, and I had pretty much given the Old Man (winter) another day.

My customary evening walk along the road to the marsh offered some incontrovertible phenological signals. The marsh edge glowed with red maple buds bursting into flower. Two eastern phoebes foraged low to the ground among the reeds, bills snapping audibly on the first emerging insects. As night fell, the woodcock danced and sang with enthusiasm, it seemed to me, unequaled on previous nights.

One voice was missing, however, a voice so obviously tied to things vernal that, to human ears, that voice cries but one word: "Spring ... Spring ... Spring ..."

I am always amazed that a ,3/4 inch treefrog's note is so loud and clear and full of import.

Few people have seen the spring peeper, but many know his call.

The peepers know when spring has come. They lie for the winter under the dank forest litter, their body fluids like molasses, sometimes literally frozen in ice crystals inhibited only by natural anti-freezes such as glucose. Finally, the first warm spring rains stir them to the surface, where they begin the trek to their breeding areas. Some begin calling even before they reach the water.

The first one I heard on March 15 was doing just that, hap-pily voicing his opinion of the changing weather from a rela-tively dry woodland grove 100 yards from the marsh. Others had already reached the water and stationed themselves on the perimeter, albeit calling slowly, but calling nonetheless. A month from now, the chorus would be so loud and enthusiastic that individual peeper voices would be lost in the din. Human calendar dates aside, these first voices brought official spring.

Except for their calls, spring peepers live inconspicuous lives. Even highly skilled herpetologists seldom encounter peepers outside of the spring breeding season. Contrary to the tree frog image, peepers spend their lives close to the forest floor, rarely more than 3 or 4 feet off the ground. I found one in a hemlock grove in Stokes Forest one August, quite by accident. When I finally managed to capture the tiny leaping frog, I was surprised to find telltale crossing lines on its gray-brown back. This one must have been a female, because she was a good inch and a quarter long.

Springtime peepers are easier to find, especially at night with the aid of a flashlight, but don't let anyone tell you it's easy. The ventriloqual voices madden the searcher. The best peeper-finding technique requires a warm night, a willing partner, hip boots, and two good flashlights. Good breeding sites are easily found via the chorusing voices. Peepers breed both at temporary ponds and small permanent water bodies.

At the breeding site, try to single out one individual and move closer to it from opposite sides. When you and your companion are reasonably close to the frog, both shine your flashlights where you think its call is coming from. Where the beams cross is the place to start looking. If the peeper you are searching for suddenly quiets down, he can often be induced to vocalize again with a skillfully whistled imitation of his call. Sometimes peepers will continue to call even while a light is on them.

A male peeper defends a small territory at the breeding site. His calls attract females. The basis for a female peeper's choice of mates is not well known, although the vocal abilities of her prospective mate certainly play a role. When a female finds the male she wants, she approaches and makes contact with him. They then join in amplexus (frog sex), when the male clasps the female from behind, and move to the water, where the female extrudes her eggs singly or in small groups, and the male fertilizes them. A single female may lay as many as one thousand eggs.

After amplexus and egg-laying, the female leaves the water for a solitary summer in damp woodlands. The male returns to his calling perch and awaits another female.

Spring peeper eggs hatch in about a week. The dark tan tadpoles are very tiny, and can be remarkably abundant in marshes and temporary ponds. As with all other frogs, spring peeper tadpoles are fed on heavily by a host of predators, from fish to insects. Sometimes they can be found in the grips of predaceous water beetles, which incidentally are not above issuing humans a nasty bite.

Surviving peeper tadpoles metamorphose into froglets in about seven weeks, depending on water temperature, and leave the water shortly thereafter. Those tadpoles spawned in temporary water bodies must metamorphose on time, because they run the risk of being stranded in the receding ponds if they do not.

By late summer, all spring peepers have returned to the woodlands, where they forage on insects. In October, I occasionally hear solitary peeper calls deep in the woods, as though the males are reminiscing about the past spring, or hoping for the next. Individual peepers can live at least three years.

Late November normally finds all peepers under the forest litter once again, where they will remain, still and silent, until the time comes to signal spring once again.

It's been a long day

When I stepped out the back door this morning a cardinal sang lustily from the top of the birch near the pond, and a killdeer flew over, crying its way north.

Spring, that wonderful season of changes, is coming. In its early stages, spring moves oh-so-slowly, but inexorably. The days are much longer now. The sun rises just a little past 6 o'clock, and sets past 6 o'clock as well. Our days, then, are near the 12-hour length of those in the tropics, where constant day length is the rule. We passed the dark days of winter, and are headed for the time when it will be light at 5 a.m. and stay light until near 9 p.m.

As the seasons turn, the daily periods of light and darkness change, and this changing day length provides the stimulus for many natural events. Day length influences the production of hormones and enzymes, which in turn influences the growth and behavior of animals.

Biologists prove that day length affects the seasonal behavior of animals by conducting laboratory experiments in which a particular organism is subjected to a carefully controlled regime of light and dark. In this way, a biologist can mimic a particular time of year, making it spring in winter, or autumn in spring.

More than 70 years ago, the journal Nature published a study in which a scientist named W.R. Rowan caused dark-eyed juncoes to enter breeding condition out of season by exposing them to daily increasing amounts of light. Juncos, which are common at local feeders in winter, normally breed in spring and early summer, like nearly all North American birds.

Hundreds of other studies since show that the effects of day length on animals are far-ranging. Lengthening days cause the onset of the breeding cycle of some fish, similar to the pattern seen in birds. Conversely, shortening days cue white-tailed deer to breed, while, in spring, antler growth is also initiated by changing day length, this time increasing. Day length strongly influences bird migration in both spring and fall.

Before fall, many insects enter a resting stage called diapause the stage in which they will spend their winter. Shortening days are a very important "warning sign" to these insects, because if forced to wait for a cold snap to know that winter was on its way, they might be frozen dead before they found a sheltered location to spend the winter.

Of course, seasonal patterns in animals and plants are influenced by more than just the length of the day. Day length is assisted by the interaction of light, moisture and temperature. Right now, some 70-degree, sunny days would be welcome!

Waterthrush heaven

Ken Lockwood Gorge rivals heaven for a trout fisherman ... or a Louisiana waterthrush.

The gorge is beautiful. The picturesque South Branch of the Raritan River flows past hemlock-studded banks. The clear water rushes over elephantine boulders and under weathered gray logs.

The gorge, in northern Hunterdon County, is famous for its trout fishing. Innumerable fly fisherman wade the rocky river bed, looking at once like laboratory technicians, anglers, and participants in an amphibious landing of Marines. Fly-fishermen take their fun seriously; I know, because I am one. I wonder how many fly-fishermen know about the waterthrushes.

Ken Lockwood Gorge provides perfect habitat for a bird that likes to eat insects alongside moving water, which is exactly what the Louisiana waterthrush is and does.

Waterthrushes are members of the wood-warbler clan, but think they are something else. They bob and teeter at the edge of the river, or on rocks in mid-stream, behaving very much like small sandpipers. Waterthrushes eat aquatic and terrestrial insects, mollusks, small crustaceans like freshwater shrimp, and even occasional small fish trapped in shallow backwaters.

So attached to the water is the waterthrush that it often builds its nest within a meter of the stream's edge. The bird even constructs a ramp, made of leaves, leading from its nest to the water!

Louisiana waterthrushes are brown above and streaked below, obscure coloration typical for a bird that does not want to be seen. Indeed, the waterthrush's cryptic markings make the species a challenge to the birder. All obscurity disappears, however, when the bird throws back its head and sings.

A waterthrush's song descends in a rush of ringing notes, a

perfect companion voice to flowing water. The song begins with three clear whistles, falling in pitch to a cluster of tinkling notes best compared, perhaps, to the sound of a fine wine glass shattering. As warbler songs go this one is loud, no doubt because the singer's voice must carry over that of the rushing stream.

The waterthrush's song serves as a fine herald of spring's arrival, because the bird arrives in our area faithfully in the first week of April. Our waterthrushes winter thousands of miles south, in Costa Rica or perhaps as far away as Peru.

Ken Lockwood is far from the only place to find Louisiana waterthrushes nesting along its banks. The Musconetcong River has them, as do the Lockatong, the Harihokake and the Nishisakawick creeks, all in Hunterdon.

If there is a clear, flowing run nearby, you will likely find this fine singer, if you take the time to look and listen.

Cardinal virtues

The fool cardinal is at it again. Every morning there he is, crashing repeatedly into the window, red feathers flying. He'll rest for a minute, glaring in at me, then go on thumping with renewed vigor.

Wait a minute. "Glaring in at me" is not right. The cardinal definitely glares – I know a bird glare when I see one. The object of his anger, however, is what he sees when he looks at the window pane: a red bird, with a big orange bill – "What an ugly brute," thinks the cardinal – that mimics his every move. In other words, the bird sees his reflection, and intently defends his territory ... from himself.

Yet how territorial can cardinals be when 10, 20, or even more can peacefully feed together at the same feeder?

Cardinals are indeed territorial. Just ask the bird slamming into my window every morning. However, like most birds, cardinals are territorial primarily with respect to their breeding areas and mostly during breeding season. At a bird feeder, or in a good feeding area, cardinals will often eat quietly together in flocks of five, 10 or even 20 more. If food resources are abundant, cardinals have no reason to defend them. Further, in severe winter weather, cardinals cannot afford to waste energy chasing each other around.

Come springtime, a cardinal's mood changes. He begins staking out a territory, challenging all intruders. Now the cardinal tries to establish an area where he has exclusive rights to food for himself, his mate and his potential offspring. He also wants to keep other male cardinals away from his mate. This is most often the time people observe cardinals fighting with windows, shiny hubcaps, and car rearview mirrors.

Cardinals are more prone than most birds to be territorial year-round because they do not migrate. Thus, cardinals display occasional territorial behavior throughout fall and winter, and cardinals sometimes sing during all seasons.

A cardinal's song, and bird songs in general, are anything but gentle, sweet sounds offered by our feathered friends on calm sunny mornings. Bird song is first of all an outright threat of violence. "Cross this line and you've had it, buddy," whistles the cardinal from his perch in the rose bush.

Birds also sing to attract mates. In some species, males with large song repertoires are more successful attracting females. This is probably because a male that sings often, loud, and with varied phrases is more effective at repulsing competitors, making the female's chance for producing offspring greater. Females selecting good singers for mates will reproduce more successfully.

Of course, the cardinal's song still sounds sweet and happy to human ears, no matter what he is really saying.

Fox at night

I happened to be in the garage oiling the gunnels on my canoe at 4 a.m. this morning when the high-pitched, squalling barks of a red fox came floating across the countryside. Don't ask why I was up at 4 a.m. fooling with a canoe; keeping weird hours is a naturalist's prerogative, and besides, if I hadn't been up and out, I wouldn't have heard the barking and you'd be stuck reading the classifieds or something instead of reading about a warm fuzzy animal.

Based on the volume of the animal's barks, which seemed to echo from one side of the garage to the other, the fox barked quite close by. This surprised me, because no foxes had jumped through the headlights of the car or left tracks by the stream in quite some time.

In August or September, a new fox in the area would not be unusual at all, because by that time the young have pretty much gone off on their own, and often disperse from the area they were born, sometimes traveling 50 miles or more from their home den before settling down. In April, however, foxes should either already have a den with their four to nine young in it, or at least be "expecting." At this season, foxes seldom stray outside the square mile surrounding their den site.

Almost certainly, the barking fox had resided nearby for quite some time and had merely eluded detection, something red foxes are particularly good at. Perhaps he barked to his mate back at the den, letting her know that he had just caught dinner, maybe a mouse or rabbit. For the first few days after the kits are born, the female fox, or vixen, remains with them at the den and the male fox brings food to her. In only a couple of weeks, the female joins the male on hunting forays, leaving the kits in the den.

After barking four or five times, the fox fell silent, leaving me to wonder where its den might be. Red foxes ordinarily den in holes on well-drained, wooded hillsides, either digging their own burrow or, more commonly I think, modifying an old woodchuck burrow. They usually prepare more than one den site, sometimes spreading several along the same hillside, so they can quickly move their kits if their initial den site is disturbed.

I decided that, unless a late snow fell for tracking, the chances of finding the den were slim at best. Probably I would be wise not to disturb the den anyway. I will just watch for the young foxes when the time comes for them to begin hunting this summer.

Skunk Cabbage

I went looking for early spring wildflowers one March day, but came up almost empty. Not a single trout lily, spring beauty, or marsh marigold enlivened the gray-brown landscape. All I could find were flowers and leaf buds of everyone's favorite plant – skunk cabbage.

Skunk cabbage leaf buds are green and pointy, and as they emerge from the marsh muck they begin to unfurl and look like rolled-up leaves, which is exactly what they are.

Skunk cabbage flowers offer less a sign of spring than the leaves, because often the flower buds begin to protrude from the ground in late autumn. The flowers themselves are not visible at this time; a mottled red and green structure called a spathe encases them. When spring rolls around, one side of the spathe opens and exposes the round pod-like flower cluster.

Skunk cabbage cheats its way to the surface, often growing right through a frost layer or through snow. It does this by creating heat. Imagine, a warm-blooded plant! When air temperatures approach freezing, the flower burns oxygen at a rate approaching that of a hummingbird, and the flower may actually feel warm to the touch. The maximum body temperature of a skunk cabbage flower is about 70 degrees, and it is theorized that this warmth accelerates the development of flower and fruit, as well as making pollination easier for bees and other pollinators in cold spring weather.

I love to lead kindergarten children on a spring nature walk and offer them a piece of skunk cabbage to sniff. "Yuk!" is the typical response, although about one in 10 people find the smell of the huge, bright green leaves pleasant. To me, they smell more like cabbage than skunk. The smell is caused by a chemical called calcium oxalate, which in addition to being odoriferous is quite caustic if ingested. Or so I have read, not being too eager to try some myself.

One thing that is apparent is the skunk cabbage plant's resistance to insects and herbivorous mammals. Nothing eats the stuff, save black bears, and so skunk cabbage thrives in nearly any swamp or floodplain in the region. Wherever the ground stays damp, skunk cabbage will grow.

In late summer, skunk cabbage begins to die back, and by November almost no sign of the plant is in evidence. However, through winter and spring, skunk cabbage does an important job. Although the leaves die off, skunk cabbage is actually a long-lived perennial with tough, worm-like roots spreading from the central stem. These roots are important in holding wetland soil in place during flood periods. An individual skunk cabbage plant might survive floods and droughts for many decades, and so can prevent soil erosion that might otherwise befoul streams and deplete wetland wildlife havens.

So the plant is good, even if it doesn't smell that way.

Wildflowers

A special group of wildflowers is available right now for study, or just soul rejuvenation, in the woodlands and along the forested streamsides of our area. These species are known as the "spring ephemerals," because they flower and set seed even before the trees fully leaf out. The most common spring ephemerals in our area are trout lily, bloodroot, spring beauty, rue anemone, and marsh marigold.

By sprouting and blooming so early, these flowers beat trees to the punch – or rather, to the sunlight. In summer, shade from tall trees reduces the amount of direct sunlight reaching the forest floor by as much as 90 percent, making growth difficult for flowering plants. The spring ephemerals take advantage of a narrow window of time when surface frost is gone, temperatures moderate, but shade is not a problem. This window opens for about a month and a half, from late March through early May.

Marsh marigold, a pretty buttercup-like flower, grows only in wetlands, as its name implies. Trout lily, which also goes by the names dogtooth violet and yellow adder's tongue, may be named partially from its habit of growing along streamsides. In bloom, trout lily sports a lovely, nodding yellow flower, but the plant can easily be identified by its leaves alone, which are green with brown mottling in a pattern remarkably like that of a brook trout's back.

Bloodroot, spring beauty and rue anemone are all white flowers of medium-wet to moderately dry woodlands.

Bloodroot, which has dark green leaves clasping the stem, commonly grows on slopes or even roadside embankments. This small but showy flower is wonderfully abundant right now along Mountain Road in my hometown of East Amwell. Bloodroot apparently gets its name from the red juice in its roots.

Spring beauty's small white flowers have white petals with pink lines on them, and the plant's leaves resemble grass. This is a very abundant flower, often growing in sparse clusters a few feet around. Spring beauty is supposed to have an edible tuber, though I've never had the heart to dig up the pretty little plants to try it.

Rue anemone's flowers remind me of a star, with green leaves symmetrically arranged directly under the flower. This species is quite delicate looking, balanced on what seems to be a spindly stem.

These flowers, plus one or three others, comprise nearly all the species the average person will find in bloom in April. If you take a few minutes to learn them, you can really impress your friends by confidently naming every flower you see in the average April woodland. Most other common species, like asters, goldenrods and daisies, wait until summer to bloom. They can afford to, because these species grow in open meadows and on unshaded roadsides, where there is much less competition for sunlight.

Spring is here, the grass is riz ... and for right now, the woods is where the flowers is.

Fish hawks

A remarkable natural event occurred on Palm Sunday, an event I observed from my north Hunterdon home but one that probably was in progress throughout New Jersey and Pennsylvania. Ospreys by the dozens migrated overhead.

Ospreys are large, highly migratory birds of prey, sometimes known as fish hawks. The birds flying on Palm Sunday certainly spent their winter south of the Mexican border, possibly as far south as Patagonia. Their destination, not to be reached for many days, might be Quebec, Ontario or northeastern New England.

The nasty, cloudy and cold weather system of the weekend finally blew out by mid-afternoon on Sunday, replaced by sunshine and strong west winds. Although ospreys had been casually passing over for several days, the poor weather created a bird traffic jam of sorts to our south, and the clearing weather turned the light green for the birds to continue north. Between 4 and 5 p.m. I counted more than 28 ospreys, along with a dozen other birds of prey, as they glided north.

One of the ospreys paused for a fish snack, hovering over my pond for a moment before plunging in feet-first. Fishing is the osprey specialty, and they have perfected the art. They even know how to compensate for the water's light refraction! I was not at all surprised when the bird came up with a 7-inch bass locked in its talons – although the bass probably was.

Ospreys are often seen "packing a lunch" while migrating, apparently intending to eat when they are done flying for the day. The bird at my pond did not linger to dine, but continued north with his fish.

Ospreys will continue passing over this region through early May, stopping occasionally to fish at ponds, reservoirs and rivers. Although they are a threatened species in New Jersey, the birds can be found in good numbers along the Atlantic and Delaware Bay coasts, where they construct large stick nests on trees, on high-tension towers, and on special platforms erected for them. Formerly they may also have nested inland in the state, but other than one or two pairs on the Delaware River, none still do.

Moving with the ospreys that Sunday were about 10 American kestrels. These small falcons often perch near fields or along roadways, where they scan for their prey. During the winter, kestrels feed on mice and sometimes birds, while in the summer they prefer grasshoppers and other large insects.

Unlike ospreys, kestrels frequently nest in this area. One pair usually nests in a hole in a dead branch of a large oak just north of Pittstown. The birds often hover over fields as they search for prey.

The Shad run

Before long the shad run will be in full swing. Fisherman will line the banks of the Delaware, and on weekends popular spots will be so thick with boats that you could walk across the river on them. Fishermen catch more than 50,000 shad annually in the Delaware.

All this is very interesting, and not just for fishermen. The American shad as a wildlife species has a fascinating life history. The species earns its nickname of "poor man's salmon" by being anadromous, just as salmon are. The shad ascending the Delaware are leaving the ocean to spawn, generally depositing their eggs from Belvidere north to the forks of the Delaware. Unlike salmon, a significant number of shad survive spawning and return to sea.

In only a few days juvenile shad hatch from the eggs. They grow into "fry" in their natal areas, and move south towards Delaware Bay and the Atlantic in August, when they are about 2 inches long.

While at sea, shad feed on plankton and tiny crustaceans. After entering the river, shad stop eating, but like salmon can be enticed to strike an artificial lure.

Before first spawning, and between spawns for surviving

adults, shad range widely in the Atlantic. Some individuals swim more than 2,500 miles in a year. The shad's tendency to roam is largely due to its sensitivity to ocean temperature. Shad like their water between 55 and 65 degrees Fahrenheit, and while in the ocean seek areas in this temperature range. Most Atlantic shad migrate to in the Bay of Fundy region in August and September, because this is the only place at that time of year with the shad's preferred water temperature.

Most people think of bald eagles or peregrine falcons as indicators of environmental quality. American shad also prove to be excellent indicators of the health of their environment. At one time, shad spawned in at least 19 New Jersey rivers, including the Hackensack and the Raritan. Pollution, channel alteration and dams have destroyed the runs in all but the Delaware, and in fact the Delaware run was nearly lost as well.

By the early 1900s, the Delaware shad runs were almost a memory. The fish simply could not make it through the pollution blocks at Camden and Philadelphia. During the 1940s airplane pilots nearing Philadelphia were advised not to become alarmed at the stench from the river, which, it is said, could be detected at 5,000 feet. Happily, the river is no longer used as a sewer, although municipal sewer systems still discharge treated wastes into the river, and runoff carries other pollutants.

Overall, the modern-day Delaware runs pretty clean (I swim in it regularly each summer), and the shad run increases every year. Which is a happy thing, whether you cast for shad, sample their fillets at the Lambertville Shad Festival, or just like to know that there is still hope for the environment.

Encounter with a treefrog

A gray treefrog called loudly from a large mud puddle in the front of Delaware Township School the other night, so loudly he actually startled my son Tim and me as we walked back to the car after watching Tim's brother's Little League game. The school has construction going on, and the little muddy pool the frog chose could not have been there very long.

It seemed like a surprising place to encounter one of these treefrogs, but then gray treefrogs have been known to breed in stranger locations. A friend, for example, once found dozens of gray treefrog tadpoles in his above-ground swimming pool.

Gray treefrog tadpoles are easily recognized by their green body and red tail. When they first transform into adult frogs, gray treefrogs are a brilliant bright green color. As they mature, the color changes to the gray they are named for.

Gray treefrogs usually do not begin calling until nighttime temperatures reach 50 degrees, although they have a remarkable ability to withstand cold winter temperatures. Researchers have proven that they can survive for several days, partially frozen at a temperature of 20 degrees!

The most likely place for the average person to see a gray treefrog is on a window. As on all treefrogs, enlarged suction cup-like pads tip each toe on this species, making climbing a smooth vertical surface simple. Gray treefrog toe pads are larger than those of most treefrogs.

Windows are prime foraging sites for these frogs, because on warm summer nights a house window with a light on inside attracts hundreds of insects. The frog climbs the house and perches "stuck" to the window pane, toe pads adhering to the glass, until a bug flies within range. Keep an eye on your windows this summer; if the frogs are in the area, they will show up eventually.

Gray treefrogs are large for treefrogs, reaching almost 2 inches long. They are variably colored and mottled on their backs in shades of gray, with a bit of vibrant yellow-orange color on the underside of each hind leg. This splash of color is termed flash coloration, and helps keep the frogs from becoming food for something else. When a predator approaches, the frog leaps away, exposing briefly the bright color. The color theoretically both startles the would-be predator and gives it a search image to pursue. When the frog lands, its legs fold again and the color disappears, and to the predator, so does the frog.

The call of this species is a very loud trill; a chorus of them around a breeding pond can be almost deafening, blocking out all nearby sounds. The one at the school was especially effective in his vocal efforts to attract a mate, because his voice was echoing off the brick school walls.

Keep an eye on your windows and an ear out for their explosive trilling, and maybe you will run across one of these interesting little animals.

Snappers on the move

Why does the snapping turtle cross the road? Who knows? But don't stand too close if you find one.

Actually, snapping turtles seldom leave the muddy ponds and streams they call home. When they do, they are either traveling to a different pond, or looking for sandy or gravely places to lay their eggs.

Unlike many other turtles, snapping turtles are thriving, and can be found in nearly any pond or slow stream. For the most part they are quite secretive, staying close to the bottom and feeding on aquatic insects, fish, frogs, and occasional ducklings or small mammals.

Snapping turtles are very much out of their element on dry land. Like all turtles, they are slow. Snappers also have a very small lower shell, leaving their bottoms open to attack. (The small lower shell, together with the snapper's saw-toothed tail, identify the species.) This does not matter when they are on the muddy bottom of a pond, but on land it is a different story.

In April, male snapping turtles begin seeking mates, and may travel to other ponds looking for one. Females are ready to lay their eggs in late May or June, and frequently can be found wandering about looking for the right spot. The female often selects a sandy roadside, railway embankment, or other human-made spot to deposit her 25 or so ping-pong ball-sized eggs. The sand pits used for throwing horseshoes at one of Hunterdon County's parks are annually used by a snapper.

The size and ferocity of snapping turtles are the stuff of legends. People frequently tell tales of snapping turtles measuring

3 feet across. My father used to tell, with a twinkle in his eye, about the time a friend of his stepped on a rock while fishing and was carried off – the rock, of course, being a giant snapping turtle.

These legends have some basis in fact. Snapping turtles can live more than 40 years, and do reach impressive sizes. The largest I ever measured spanned 18 inches front to back along its shell, but even larger ones have been found, including one that weighed 47 pounds. With such size, and with their namesake jaws, snapping turtles do seem intimidating, but they are always more eager to avoid a fight than start one.

Snapping turtles in the water actually shy away from people, tucking their heads into their shells. On land, however, they are put on the defensive. Like mammals and birds, snapping turtles bite in defense when they are cornered. A big one can even snap a broomstick in two with its jaws, but it would not be a threat to a smart human for one simple reason: A smart human would not corner a snapping turtle!

The grass isn't always greener

Boy, it's green around here.

That was the first thing I noticed when I returned from Arizona, where I camped, hiked and watched birds throughout what many biologists consider the most fascinating area in the United States. Exploring the Sonoran desert and the mountains southeast of Tucson felt very new and different from walking the green hills of Hunterdon County.

Southeast Arizona is renowned for its biological diversity. More different kinds of nesting birds, for example, pack into this relatively small area than in any comparably sized place in the United States. I saw more than 200 species of birds on my trip, and close to 500 species have been recorded in the region. Many of these species can be found nowhere else in North America north of Mexico.

One of the first questions my birder friend Chris asked on my return was, "How many 'lifers' did you get?" The answer is that a staggering 111 new bird species wound up on my life list thanks to this trip.

Gambel's quail called and barrel cacti stabbed in the desert. Swainson's hawks hunted over the grasslands. Elegant trogons, more colorful than parrots, greeted us in the mountain canyons, with fantastic rock formations and ancient petroglyphs in the background. I chased after a rattlesnake in one canyon to take its picture.

When we first arrived in Arizona, the atmosphere sparkled so clearly we could see The Milky Way as a broad white stripe through the night sky. By the end of the trip smoke from forest fires had clouded the skies and obscured even nearby mountain peaks.

Four major biogeographical regions, or biomes, are packed into southeastern Arizona: the Rocky Mountains, the Sierra Madre Mountains, the Chihuahuan Desert and the Sonoran Desert. Elevation ranges from 2,300 feet in the desert to nearly 10,000 feet in the mountains. On many days, we spent the cool mornings in the desert, but enjoyed 60 degree temperatures at midday in the higher regions, while the desert broiled in a heat wave that pushed daytime temperatures past 100.

What did I get out of the trip to southeastern Arizona, besides a bunch of new birds, and a tan? Believe it or not, I gained a new appreciation for New Jersey.

I was certain on the flight out that Arizona far surpassed my home state in all respects, but once there I recognized that New Jersey's lush forests, green farmlands, salt marshes, and sandy beaches are unique and precious in their own right.

One morning, we hiked through Cave Creek Canyon, supposedly the best birding spot in Arizona. We found many fantastic birds, such as glowing red-faced warblers, colorful painted redstarts, and a pair of elegant trogons.

I remarked to my companion, however, that we would easily have seen more species, and some just as beautiful and fascinating, on a hike in any New Jersey forest.

I guess the grass is green enough right here.

Northbound migrants

The bird's strident calls nearly knocked me off my mountain bike. Few animals vocalize as emphatically as a startled gray catbird – or, for that matter, a startled naturalist.

I was out on a "see who's back today" ride, peddling through the predawn half-light on a twisty gravel back road, binoculars around my neck and ears tuned to hear newly arrived spring migrant birds. The catbird caught me by surprise when he let loose from the roadside thicket; he was a few days early and plenty loud.

The date was April 24, and several other "new" birds let me know that spring is here. A wood thrush called from a wooded knoll, while farther back in the woods a scarlet tanager sang. Chimney swifts sought insects over the one lake on my morning bike route, and a spotted sandpiper searched for insect larvae in the mud along the banks.

Nearly every day for the next few weeks we can hope for new returnees from the South. Some birds will be traveling from the relatively close southeastern United States, while others will come thousands of miles, all the way from South America.

Most song-birds inhabiting our woods and fields migrate at night. This comes as a surprise to many people, but if you think about it, flying at night makes perfect sense. Nocturnal migrants take advantage of the darkness to avoid predators like sharp-shinned hawks, and avoid wasting precious daylight hours that could be used for feeding.

If the weather is favorable, birds like thrushes, tanagers and warblers will take off shortly after sundown, ascend from several hundred to a few thousand feet, and fly northward all night. On a big migration night, calls from dozens of birds can be heard from the ground as they pass over, and a telescope trained on the moon often reveals the shadows of passing birds.

When daylight approaches, the birds descend and begin searching for favorable habitat. They deplete a large portion of their energy reserves during a nocturnal flight, and must feed immediately to restore them. Birds may linger in a suitable spot for a few days, or they may depart after only one day of resting and feeding. Thus, the migration proceeds in a sort of leapfrog fashion: songbirds cover one hundred miles or more in a night, pause for a day or two, and move on again.

There is a flaw in this strategy, a flaw that a thousand years ago did not really matter. The strategy assumes that, when the birds land, there will be a place for them to feed. Most species of songbirds are declining in numbers, and loss of habitat is the major reason why.

If a migrating bird ends his night flight over a forested park in Hunterdon County, no problem. But imagine one of these birds descending from nocturnal migration over Newark, N.J.. The bird is exhausted, and desperately needs to feed, but there are no trees in sight. What to do? Well, hopefully the bird would be able to muster enough energy to fly around until it finds a city park to feed in.

Or the bird might very well die.

Not enough time

I don't have enough time right now. I mean, I never have enough time, but never is the passage of time so evident as it is in May. Something changes or something's new every time you blink your eyes, or go to sleep ... or go to work.

Trees leaf out rapidly. The leaves, which spent the winter packaged in miniature within the buds, now unfurl, revealing that wonderful light spring green.

Fern fiddleheads uncurl in the low places, in the spring seeps on the mountainsides, and even in dry places, because not all ferns prefer moist soil. Fiddleheads are nothing more (or less) than new spring growth pressing skyward; they get their name because they look like the head of a fiddle. Cinnamon ferns, New York ferns, ostrich ferns – I wish I knew them all.

Amidst the ferns might be a mud-covered box turtle just emerged from her hibernaculum, or maybe a wood frog, with its bold black eye stripe.

Butterflies with magical colors appear from nowhere. They have magical names, as well: tiger swallowtail, painted lady, spring azure, monarch. Mourning cloaks have been out for several weeks already, of course.

There are so many places to be in May. I want to be in an old apple orchard, seeing and smelling the clouds of white blossoms, and listening for the chatter of a Wilson's warbler. Meadows are special now, too, with the newly arrived bobolinks back from South America, and even, in a few, select places, the upland sandpipers.

The forests are richly alive in May. No habitat in the world equals the flush of plant growth that occurs in a May woodland, and the flush of insect activity accompanying it. This is why May is such a great bird month in our area; birds time their migration to hit the peak time for insect availability. While patrolling the woods for birds, I might be lucky enough to find a pink lady's slipper in bloom.

Now is also the time to head for the southern coast of New Jersey, where thousands of shorebirds stop to feed in the rich coastal marsh before continuing the journey to their Arctic nesting grounds. My wife and I spent our honeymoon in Cape May in May, and in my mind's eye I can still see the gleaming white and black plumage of the black-bellied plovers on the marshes of Stone Harbor, bathed in the red light of the setting sun.

The chuck-will's-widows and whip-poor-wills are calling in south Jersey now, too, and I fondly remember their calls as well.

So many places, so many flowers, so many birds ... so little time. Every spring I try to go everywhere at once, and every spring I miss something. That is no reason to stop trying – after all, I only have a few dozen more Mays left, and I can't afford to waste even one.

Growing up

A blond mayfly dun lifts from its trip down the evening river, drifts across the gravel beach, and alights next to my plate. It is tiny, about a size 18 to a fly-fisherman, and very pretty actually, with three long tails arching up behind it.

I stare numbly at the insect for several minutes.

The mayfly does not speak. It does not whine, throw Styrofoam cups on the ground, play loud music, or ignore me when I make the simple request, "Stay right there for a minute."

In other words, the likes of it I have not seen in several days. Or maybe I have.

The mayfly cooperates by staying right where it is, a very nice gesture to a tired paddler. Mayflies do not have much time to waste. Nature grants most mayfly species only a day in which to dry the amnion from their wings, flutter about looking for a mate, set down on the river and lay eggs ... and float downstream, to die. Every mayfly treats its first river trip as its last. Perhaps that is how it had been for the city kids now scattered on the bank around me. I am not sure if the city grown-ups understood as well as the kids, or as well as the mayfly.

We began up north three days ago, launching squadrons of heavy, sluggish, but unbreakable plastic canoes, 60 boats and 120 never-paddled-befores strong. I was assigned – well, actually, I was asked – to serve as part of the crew of safety patrollers and general on-the-water whip crackers for the expedition. I knew most of the canoe leaders by experience and the rest by reputation: crusty veterans of many a trip.

The off-the-water whip crackers were teachers and a school principal from the city, who arranged the trip, the camping sites, the food, the transport of gear, and the evening activities.

It seemed like a good deal for us canoe leaders. The trip was an excuse for three days out of the office. The trip organizers had a truck to haul gear from campsite to campsite, meaning we could paddle lightened boats. We were to be responsible only when the group was on the water, and on land left to our own devices, meaning story-telling spiced by firewater, and, trip veterans rumored, catered meals.

After stowing my paddling gear in a borrowed plastic slug, I walked about at the launch site, eavesdropping. The adults, still in the city, were tense and authoritative, while the kids bantered happily. The scene reminded me of a passage I once read about growing up, written by North Country canoeing sage Sigurd Olson. Sig pointed his pen at these kids, or rather the grownups guiding them.

He wondered whether growing up was not a process of growing down, a process whereby people lose their awareness and joy as they age. I think it would be better to be a mayfly. Grope about the river bottom dodging trout as an ugly nymphal child, but always look forward to that river trip, with its sights and sounds and even death.

Then a pair of teen-aged boys dragged their canoe across a gravel road and down the cement boat ramp, and shoved it into the water. Someone had given the order, and off we went.

Now already the trip has ended, the mayfly rests, and I enjoy a catered barbecue on the river gravel beach aptly named Point Pleasant. The caterers serve remarkably posh food for canoe-camping, as they have done for the whole trip. The kids, however, seem to prefer shoveling down hamburgers and hot dogs, anyway, rather than following their teachers' lead with barbe-cued beef, barbecued chicken, fancy potato salad, and so forth.

Hoping to remain neutral, I gobble both hamburgers and barbecued beef, and just about everything else. Replete with food and drink, I sit watching our mayfly and recovering from the three days of high school children who displayed the usual teen-aged difficulty in following simple instructions, like "Put your hand on top of the paddle" or "Please put the trash in the trash bag" or "Please keep your canoe in this pool until everyone's boat is on the water," and who seemed to reserve their energy for high jinks instead of paddling.

And recovering from watching them listen to the periodic harangues of their elders, though the devil consoles me by saying, "At least they didn't listen too hard."

I wonder if the school staff sitting with me at the table would appreciate the mayfly. I decide they would, and lift my hand to point to the insect about the same time a teacher returns to the table with a plate full of creme puffs and other desserts. I stay my hand, and she sets the plate down.

Right down on the blond mayfly, thus ending its river trip.

———

Christina, one of the 26 teen-agers in group "B," the pod I coaxed and cajoled down the river, walks over to me with her hand outstretched, palm up. She is a small girl, and very pretty, actually, with a naturally graceful walk.

"I have a blister." Christina says with a smile.

"How about that," I say, trying to smile back. Christina is not such a bad kid. None of them are really bad kids, especially considering that they live in Manhattan.

"I've never had one before."

"How about that!"

Christina walks off, and my gaze returns to the table, and I am glad that I have the hope of going down the river again, and I wish I had shown Christina the mayfly.

Hummers

From May onward is the time to be watching flower beds for two fascinating visitors. This is especially so if coral-bells, butterfly-weed, zinnias, and other nectar-rich flowers can be counted among the blooms. Hummingbirds and look-alike hummingbird moths are likely to be seen hovering in front of such plants.

The more common of the two, the moth, looks like a cross between a bird, a moth and a crayfish. Hummingbird moths behave very much like a hummingbird, hovering before plants on wings beating so rapidly they blur. Instead of a bill, the moths unroll long, hollow tongues to drink the sugary nectar.

Hummingbird moths are more properly called common clearwings. They are one of the more than 100 kinds of sphinx moths found in North America. The clearwing's larvae, a green caterpillar with red spots, feeds on several species of plants, including cherries.

The more desired visitor is, of course, the hummingbird. About 20 kinds of hummingbirds have been seen in North America, but only one is found regularly in the East. Our ruby-throated hummingbirds have just recently returned from their winter home in the tropics after a journey of more than a thousand miles. During their trip, ruby-throated hummingbirds fly nonstop across the Gulf of Mexico, a remarkable feat for a bird tiny enough to fit into a teaspoon.

Ruby-throated hummingbirds are metallic green above. Only the males have the iridescent red throat that gives the bird its name. Females and young males have whitish throats. Like other hummers, ruby-throats use their long, thin bills to consume nectar.

Although known for their nectar feeding habits, hummingbirds also eat insects and occasionally drink tree sap. Diverse eating habits are important especially to male hummingbirds, which tend to return to the north earlier than females and before most flowers are blooming. Hummers burn energy so quickly that they must consume their weight in food each day.

In cold weather, even this is not enough energy.

To conserve energy on cold nights or when food is scarce, hummingbirds become torpid during the hours of darkness. This torpid state is a kind of mini-hibernation. The hummingbird's temperature may drop from its normal 104 degrees to an incredible 54, reducing the bird's metabolic rate by one third or more!

Attracting hummingbirds and hummingbird-moths is not difficult. Hummers feed on bee-balm, cardinal flower, geranium, gladiolus and phlox, among many other garden species. Red flowers lure more hummingbirds than other colors. Sugar-water feeders are also available for the hummers.

Hummingbirds will mostly be attracted to areas around homes for a brief visit in May and again in August-September, when they are migrating. They do nest locally where suitable streamside woods can be found, however, and so in some places they may be found all summer.

World Series time

The police officer looked as tired as I felt. "Do you have any idea why I pulled you over?"

Of course, I knew the answer. I just figured that speed limits under 50 miles per hour were waived at 2 a.m.

The next question was the one I had been afraid of: "Where are you going at this time of night?"

How do you explain to someone that the reason you are speeding through a small town in the middle of the night is to get to a distant marsh before daylight so you can listen for birds that make noises in the dark?

"Officer, have you ever heard of the World Series of Birding?"

He hadn't, of course, and neither have most people. The World Series is a bird-watching competition held every year from midnight to midnight on the Saturday closest to May 15. This is the peak of spring bird migration, and teams of highly skilled birders from all over the United States, Canada and

Great Britain strive to best each other by identifying the greatest number of birds possible in New Jersey in one day.

If the weather cooperates, the winning team will have found more than 210 species of birds.

Why? Well, if you can believe it, staying up for 24 hours looking for birds is an awful lot of fun, which is reason enough. But the competition has a higher purpose. Teams seek sponsors who will pledge an amount of money per each species the team finds, just like in a walkathon. The money collected is donated to the conservation organization of the team's choice. The World Series of Birding and Birdathon raises almost half a million dollars for conservation every year. My team, the "Guerrilla Birders," is sponsored by Zeiss Optical Corporation.

Why New Jersey? Because New Jersey has an incredibly rich variety of birdlife. Few states have more different kinds of birds than New Jersey, and none has so many different kinds so close together. More than 350 occur statewide in a single year.

Most of the teams in the competition design elaborate routes through the state, visiting many prime bird areas. In 24 hours, a typical team might drive 500 or more miles. All teams must finish in Cape May by midnight.

In order to break the 200-species mark, teams must scout throughout the state before the competition to locate the more difficult-to-find species. When the policeman stopped me, I was on my way to a marsh to try to find rails, bitterns and owls, hoping to "tie them down" before the date of the competition.

Probably the most commonly asked question about the World Series of Birding is, "How do you know no one is lying about what they saw?" The answer is simple. Birders don't lie, at least not about birds.

Umbrella plants

While wandering around a forest with my kids one sunny Sunday afternoon, I noticed a familiar plant weaving a touch of spring into the still quite bare woodland.

In spring, forests turn green from the ground up, with the ephemeral spring wildflowers providing the first green. Spring ephemerals include such plants as spring beauty, trout lily and the "umbrella plants," as my 6-year old named the clump of mayapples poking through the leaves.

Umbrella plant aptly describes mayapples, or mandrakes, as they are sometimes called. As they poke through the forest floor, the plants bear an uncanny resemblance to a closed umbrella, and when the leaves unravel they seem the ideal rain protection for a frog- or salamander-sized creature. At full growth, mayapples reach 1 to 1½ feet in height.

After they fully emerge and open, mayapples bloom, with the white flower nodding inconspicuously below the leaves. As their name implies, in mid-to-late spring the flowers produce a lemon-shaped, yellowish fruit about 2 inches long. These May "apples" are supposed to be edible, though I have never tried one.

Mayapples almost always grow in clumps in their rich woods habitat, and for a good reason. Like beech trees and many other plants, mayapples spread by underground horizontal stems called rhizomes. Each plant in a clump genetically matches every other.

Spreading by rhizomes is one way for plants like mayapples to hedge their bets. It is a risky business for flowers to emerge and bloom in early spring. An unusual cold snap could kill the flowers outright, but even more importantly, the cool spring weather minimizes activity by pollinating insects like bees and flies. Spreading by rhizomes requires no pollinators, and so the plants can reproduce even if traditional means fail.

Unlike some other flowers, mayapples are generalists when it comes to what insects can pollinate them. The plants hedge their bets in this way, too, because by accepting many species of pollinators they increase their chances of normal reproduction by seed. Spring wildflowers compete with each other for pollinators, especially for bumblebees, which are among the earliest insects to become active.

Ground cover plants like mayapple, growing under a forest canopy, have little choice as to when they bloom. All plants require sunlight to grow, and, as spring progresses, less and less light will reach the forest floor. By mid-summer, only 1 percent of the sunlight striking the forest canopy will reach the ground layer.

No matter how or why they do it, I am always glad to see the first mayapples poking through and blending green into the woodland floor, although when the rush of colors comes in May, I am perhaps less apt to notice the plants on the ground.

Friendly neighborhood bears

A couple of Sundays ago, I got a phone call: "Are you the one who writes for the paper?"

"I am," I said.

"I have a bear in my backyard, and I'm not sure what I should do."

Some people have all the luck. I never get any bears in my backyard.

As it turned out, this person had exactly the right reaction to the bear. She was excited and interested and somewhat concerned about the bear's safety. She thought her neighbors might be upset if they saw a bear walking down the street.

So I said: "Just enjoy it, and keep a respectful distance. You don't need to call anybody unless you think the animal is going to cause a problem, like, for example, damaging property or trying to get into a house or shed looking for food. Then you should call state fish and game officials, or as a last resort, the local police."

Black bears, which are the only kind of bear found in the East, are not exactly uncommon in New Jersey any more, and their population is increasing. This particular individual was probably a young male. Young male bears tend to wander in springtime, looking for females. Aggressive and territorial adult males, sometimes exceeding 400 pounds, may push young males out of prime bear habitat, encouraging the wandering tendency.

It is still pretty unusual to see a black bear. I only see about one per year in New Jersey, although I frequently cross their tracks or scat when I am in Sussex County.

One reason that black bears are not often seen is that they are extremely shy, and ordinarily avoid man at all costs. In summer, they tend to be most active in the evening or at night, feeding on vegetation, wild fruits, insects, small animals and carrion. It is highly unusual for a black bear to catch and kill large prey.

Although shy, black bears are tempted by easy food. Garbage, pet food left outdoors, and food left for birds or other wild animals can attract an otherwise shy bear. Once homed in on a food handout, black bears can become nuisances, knocking over garbage cans, raiding vegetable gardens, and frightening pets or people. It is best, therefore, to avoid practices that might attract the bruins.

Phoebe Day

People are always looking for another day off, naturalist-types included. The problem for naturalists is that the days our jobs give us off are not often the ones we want off.

Just look at the list of official holidays your ever-benevolent employer scroogily allows you. The first problem, of course, is that the list could easily be written on a postage stamp. As if that's not enough, look at how the days are selected. Take Labor Day, as a randomly picked example.

This year Labor Day falls on Monday, Sept. 5. What will you do that day? Broad-wingeds won't peak for another 10 days, at least. A cold front might produce a good warbler flight, but you and I both know that if we have Sept. 5 off, the cold front will pass on Sept. 6.

How about Memorial Day weekend? May 26 to 29, a perfect time to scan the shores of Delaware Bay, filling mind and binoculars with a hundred thousand red knots ... except that 80 bazillion upholstered horseless overheating hunks from Detroit will be headed down the parkway, the turnpike, – even Route 539, for gosh sake – ruining our fun before we even get there. The traffic melting the highways rivals Fourth of July weekend.

Fourth of July. What an idiotic day to have off! Migrant songbirds are in Canada, breeding songbirds are as silent as an eighth-grader who read the wrong chapter, shorebirds only spatter the mudflats instead of paving them. The only thing worth looking at on the Fourth of July wears a bikini. At least it ain't February.

Now, I don't mind a day off in February, you understand, as long as it comes with partially frozen shore ponds and east winds sweeping rare gulls inland. Or on the flip side, if the mercury nudges 50 degrees, then maybe a brown trout could be convinced to move its lethargic body three inches into the current to inhale a pretty drowned fly with a string attached. But this is a vain hope.

Lincoln's and Washington's birthdays will be rainy, muddy, not yet spring but not quite winter, might-as-well-go-to-work-anyway days. What we need are holidays that come to us naturally.

Natural holidays oscillate, ignoring the calendar in the narrow sense but moving in a rhythmic, greater picture. You can't know the day has come until the day has come.

Natural holidays waver on the axis of a median date, sometimes running early, sometimes a little late, sometimes, depending on the holiday, skipping a year or two or 10. And never coming again, for each holiday is marked by an event that only resembles last year's, something like a child's resemblance to the parent, similar but not the same.

Which is why we cannot afford to miss them, all of them, any of them.

And so I propose that the powers that be name these holidays, and recognize them, and understand that one cannot work on such days as these. It will even help the economy, honest!

Just imagine: More days for people to buy extra groceries for parties, more miles traveled visiting, more overnight stays in motels, more presents to give, and a whole battalion of themes for the Hallmark company to put on cards, mugs, plaques, etc.

Leading hot chocolate mix makers could vie for the rights to be the official drink of First Snow of the Year Day (I hear the children cheering). Consider the sales events the four-wheel-drive dealers could run! My ears ache from the radio ads, and this is only the beginning.

We will have First Southbound Dowitcher Day, sometime in late June, to celebrate the beginning of summer's end, maybe with contests (sponsored by the makers of OFF!™) to see who could get the most greenhead flies to land on them. Or maybe the contests should be reserved for Prothonotary Warbler Song Day, and instead of greenheads the contestants could collect Cumberland County deer ticks.

On Strongest Cold Front in the Last Two Weeks of August Day, three false starts will be allowed, lest someone hold out for a stronger front and miss the best warblers. False start days will entitle workers to come in two hours late, and accrue annually if not used.

The false start rule will also apply on Broadwing Flight Day, and workers will get two days off in a row – one to watch the kettles of birds and one to allow time for the blue haze to clear from their eyes. Visine sales will triple; in fact, the presence of tank trucks of the stuff could be arranged for Hawk Mountain, Raccoon Ridge, Sunrise Mountain and Chimney Rock.

On October Blue Sky Day, the entire state will come out in costumes, but not of ghouls and witches. This isn't Halloween. Young and old, country bred and country bound, all people will don blue jeans, wool sweaters, and hiking boots (I hear L.L. Bean cheering). Such a wonderful time of year ... oh, what the hey, let's just have the whole month of October off.

Ross's Gull Day will only happen once every 20 years, and if you think Point Pleasant beach is crowded in August, wait until one of these rare wraiths finally decides to spend a few February days in and around Manasquan Inlet.

First Day When the Ocean Water is Warm Enough to Swim Day. November Most Spectacular Sunset Day. And many others, including the one day that will mark the beginning and end of the natural year. This day is already as sacred to some as Christmas, and no amount of commercialization could corrupt it.

A day will come in spring, as it does every spring, when a phoebe perches for the first time since autumn on one of the cattails by the pond. She will wag her tail jauntily as the reed bobs up and down, canting her head as she looks this way and that for food or foe.

Maybe (I hope), the phoebe will come holding the hands of a warm day and south wind and quacking wood frogs. Maybe, again, the day will make me glad for steaming mugs of soup and sorry for the poor phoebe, perched almost right on the water and hoping a damselfly nymph will swim close to the surface.

I will have my cards ready this year. I never get around to sending Christmas cards, but on First Phoebe Day the palpable joy begs to be shared with friends far away, especially friends to the north who have not found their phoebe yet.

This day will come in March, though on what day no one knows, and may be the most powerful holiday of all. First Phoebe Day is also the first day of spring, and maybe, someday, a postal worker will be glad when it has passed, not because spring is finally here, but because there will be no more stacks of Phoebe Day cards to deliver.

Summer

Alive-willet

Summer

Two frogs in a bucket

Yes, a peaceful summer evening it was, calm and free and full of promise ... of what? Maybe another encounter with sub-human life forms. I shuddered.

A few lingering rays of sunlight made patterns of bright dots and bands on the book cradled idly in my hands, highlighting the prophetic title: "Life Histories of North American Amphibians."

I lay like a hypnotized frog, on my back on the sweaty palm of the plastic recliner, gazing out through half-opened eyes while ignoring the book that could have helped me.

I was only vaguely aware of my kids and my dog, as they ran around playing and yelling excitedly about "rattlesnakes." Kids play all kinds of different games.

When the bedlam increased to tympanum-rupturing levels, I regained my wits briefly and stopped my 6-year-old as he ran by with a long piece of kindling wood with a fork on the end.

"What are you doing?"

"Gettin' th' snake!"

"Oh."

"There really is one, Daddy!"

"Uh-huh."

And back to contemplation I went. It was the frogs that had done this to me, perhaps wreaking revenge for the times when as a youngster I held them on their backs and rubbed their bellies until they lost their wits. Maybe it reached back even farther, to a time when my dad hooked frogs through the leg and cast them into ponds full of big bass.

Anyhow, I'd had a couple of run-ins with frogs recently that had not turned out as planned.

The first one started simply enough. I had a talk to do for a large gathering of Cub Scouts and Boy Scouts, and I needed something to really grab and hold their attention. What possesses enough power to capture the interest of a 9-year-old Cub Scouts and silence the sarcastic remarks of a 12-year-old Boy Scout? It needed inherent boy appeal: meaning, something that you have to catch, something hard enough to catch that it became a trophy and sign of prowess when you did. If it grossed out girls and den-leading mothers, so much the better.

The answer was simple: a frog.

The ornamental pond where I work squirms with green frogs – the species green frog, Rana clamitans – and I almost always can catch one there. So I grabbed my bucket, and a piece of burlap to put over it when I caught one, and set out.

I'll bet you're thinking "He fell in" or "He couldn't catch one." I wish it had been that easy! But I had absolutely no trouble at all catching a green frog. In fact, I caught two, one in each hand, and decided to use them both for the program. The smaller one was a male, as you would expect, with the bright yellow throat typical of male green frogs, and the enlarged thumb typical of all male frogs. There is a reason for that thumb, as you will soon see. The larger frog was the female, with a white throat.

By putting my foot through the handle and dragging it through the warm shallows, I was able to fill the bucket with water and pond scum. I shoved the frogs into the bucket, covered it quickly with the burlap, and ran a rubber band around the outside of the burlap to hold the critters in place. Happily, I set off for what I was sure would be a program the scouts would never forget.

But I had forgotten the Most Fundamental Fact of Biology – namely, what will happen if you put a boy and girl together in a warm, dark place.

With great fanfare, the boys and leaders were gathered in a circle around me and my bucket, the boys eagerly making guesses as to what lay waiting in the pail's sloshing innards while the leaders sheepishly looked away. I slipped my hand under the burlap and felt around until I touched frog, and then I grabbed and pulled and ... don't you know that that male just would not let go! The younger boys, who stood in the front so they could see better, said "Look, they're fightin'!" The older boys started roaring, and my perfect program just hopped out of reach.

The very next night, we invited friends over to go swimming and there, grinning at me from the bottom of our pool, was a big old bullfrog, large cousin of the green frog. I knew bullfrogs well. Too well. One time, one chased me away from a prime fishing hole. Don't laugh – I was only 7 years old at the time.

I had gotten permission to go fishing in the pond in back of Uncle Frank's, known lair of sunfish, and especially of giant carp. (Seven-year olds are easy to please.) So I crept to the back side of the pond, Zebco rod in hand, and before long I had a worm on the hook wishing he was somewhere else and was set to make the cast of the century. That's when the moaning howl arose from the streamside bushes: "oor RUM! ... oor oor RUM! ... oor oor RUM!!"

The thing sounded mean, whatever it was. It didn't help that I had just finished reading a book about Bigfoot in which a gold panner in California found his partner by a stream with four giant tooth marks in the back of his neck.

Luckily, humans still possess the instincts honed into their hunter-gatherer forbears over the millennia by saber-toothed tigers and cave bears. I grabbed the nearest rock and whipped it into the bushes ... and the sound stopped.

Uneasily, I continued to fish, less concerned about big carp than I was about the four holes about to gouged in my neck. Understandably, when the oor oor RUM!ing started up again, the fish must have thought they were up against nuclear-powered worms, and I know I did permanent damage to my reel's gears when I cranked the bait in and got out of there.

I was 14 when I found out bullfrogs say "oor oor RUM!" or "jug o' RUM" as it is more popularly translated. I may have subconsciously sworn revenge, but even if I hadn't, this bullfrog on the bottom of the pool was my chance to even the score with frogs.

Now, I could have been normal and scooped the softball-sized frog out with the skimmer, but I had bigger plans. I figured that if I could keep the critter moving but underwater, eventually he would run out of oxygen and I could catch him with my hands. Just think what that would do to a naturalist's reputation! I could see it plain as day – Headline: MAN OUTSWIMS FROG or FROG NO MATCH FOR WEB-FOOTED NATURALIST.

Luckily, no one had the presence of mind to run for a video camera. I have to say, I gained new respect for a frog's ability to hold his breath, although not nearly the respect my neighbors gained for my wife's ability to put up with me.

The bullfrog commanded the pool as darkness fell. Have you ever been in a pool in the dark when you know there is a big frog somewhere right next to you?

Recovering from my sad reverie, I noticed that the kids and dog had fallen strangely silent. I put my unread book aside.

Something told me I better find out about this "rattlesnake."

It was in the kitchen, backed into a corner by the circling war party of kids and dog, coiled up and ready to strike. All of 7 inches long. Its skin showed the pattern of bright dots and bands typical of a young milk snake, which is what it was.

"Hey, don't hurt that snake!" I shouted.

"Why not?" demanded my son.

I thought for a minute, and then said, "Because sometimes milk snakes eat frogs."

Empty nests

The parent Baltimore orioles were berserk, two flashes of orange diving on my uncle's Gordon setter as if intending to draw blood.

I was visiting my uncle to borrow some tool or other when the dog-bird commotion caught my eye. The orioles did not withdraw at my approach, which surprised me enough that I grabbed the dog by the collar and looked more carefully.

An odd-shaped lump at my feet shifted slightly, and in so doing transformed from the unnoticed piece of lawn debris into a baby bird doing its best to go unnoticed by a big bird dog. The young oriole had grown only about half of its feathers, and even these were not full length yet. Clearly the nestling bird had fallen or been blown from its nest.

After tying the dog, I returned to the baby bird, which began cheeping plaintively as soon as I dragged the dog off. More cheeping emanated from a nearby bush, and before I knew it I was the proud parent of three young Baltimore orioles. Except I was not the parent at all.

The real parent orioles scolded excitedly nearby, watching to see if their year's reproductive efforts were all for naught. They clearly were still interested in taking care of their young. The nestling orioles, like nearly all baby birds found on the ground, were not orphans.

This kind of thing happens all the time with birds. As baby

birds grow, the nest may become too small and one or more young may fall or be pushed out. Or a storm may rage through the area, knocking nests and nestlings to the ground. Or a nestling may decide to try to fly before it is ready, and experience an ungraceful decent to earth.

A baby bird on the ground is not doomed. Its chances for survival are reduced, of course, because it is much more vulnerable to land based predators like cats, dogs, raccoons, foxes, and ... humans.

Humans don't eat baby birds, at least not usually, but since they tend to take a grounded baby bird from its parents, they might just as well make a meal of it, too. Any baby bird's best chance to grow up as a wild, free-ranging bird is provided by its parents and living in the wild. In most cases, any help humans try to provide is only interference.

Parent birds will continue to feed fallen babies, right there on the ground. Since the babies will be "cheep-cheeping," the parents have no trouble finding them.

The main risk to a grounded baby bird is from predators. In developed areas, human-subsidized bird eaters like cats, dogs and raccoons are a particular problem.

Unless a baby bird is in immediate danger, it should be left alone. Some will die, but many will survive.

If a baby bird is in immediate danger, it can be moved to a safer location. I often suggest placing the young bird in a shoe box affixed to a tree near where it was found. The parent birds should be able to find it from its begging calls. It is fine, by the way, to gently handle baby birds. Parent birds are not put off by any scent left on the young.

Since my uncle's dog is contained by one of those invisible electric fences, I carried the three baby orioles to the edge of his property, outside the fence's boundary, where they would be safe from the setter. The parent orioles watched every step, and when I returned later to show the young orioles to my wife, Cathy, they were being actively fed by the parents.

Seventeen years

Seventeen years is a long time – a long time for humans hustling in the daylight, and a long time for an insect waiting underground.

Seventeen years ago, in 1979, I remember being out with my friend, Jimmy, snapping bushes with our swimming towels to knock the 17-year cicadas loose. We thought they were weird at best, or disgusting at worst. Unfortunately, many people still think that way of these relatively harmless insects.

I think very differently now, especially after learning more about cicadas. And, most especially, after my family and I witnessed their spectacular emergence at Jockey Hollow National Park, near Morristown.

At Jockey Hollow, dime-sized holes pocked the ground where the cicada nymphs had emerged, and dramatic humming filled the air overhead. The nymphs we found digging out of the ground had not seen sun since I was in middle school.

After falling from the trees where the eggs are laid, cicada nymphs burrow into the soil, where they remain (in this species) for 17 years. Underground, the nymphs feed on juices from tree roots, using specially adapted mouthparts.

Nymphal skins and newly emerged adults covered the trees. A quick tabulation found more than 200 on one small shrub. After doing a little math work, I realized that millions of cicadas populated the large forest at Jockey Hollow. This mass emergence overwhelms predators, assuring that most cicadas can successfully reproduce.

Awkward on their first flights, the red-eyed, 2-inch-long adults crash-landed on tree trunks, the ground, or us. Although they are big, cicadas do not bite or pinch, and my kids, my wife and I had fun letting the animals crawl around on our arms. They always crawled upward, trying to get to the top of the "tree," which is where adult cicadas go to feed on plant juices, and especially where they call for mates.

Only male cicadas call. Unlike grasshoppers and crickets, which rub wings or legs together to make sounds, a cicada vibrates two drum-like membranes on the side of its thorax, creating a hum which resonates through its hollow abdomen. Each species of cicada has a unique call.

Adults mate end-to-end. Afterward, females slit twigs and deposit eggs inside. Late in summer, look for clusters of brown leaves in oaks and hickories, because the egg-laying can kill the twigs. After hatching, the cicada nymphs fall to the ground and burrow underneath, starting the 17-year cycle over again.

Where will you be in 17 years, in the year 2013? We asked our children that as we watched the spectacle of the cicadas. The cicadas provide a time mark, unique in nature, to look back on our lives, and into the future. Enjoy them when they emerge; it will be 17 years before they appear again.

Wild strawberries

The nice thing about nature writing is that I need only take a walk to find a story.

So it was the other evening, when we were out with the kids and our new puppy. The kids, typically, foraged as we walked. Since it is June, that means wild strawberries. They found several "mother lodes," and one spot of recently disturbed, stony earth in which strawberries grew in such profusion that Donny called it the "mother, father, sister, brother and puppy lode." He suggested we pick and sell some. I suggested it might take a while to fill a pint container with raisin-sized berries. Maybe Dixie cups would be more appropriate.

The precious sweet-but-sour taste of the jewel-like fruits ended any ideas of a commercial venture. The pick- and-eat, pick-and-eat motions of the children were reminiscent, perhaps, of behaviors I envision for our hunter-gatherer ancestors.

When we got home, I read up on the strawberries, although I'm sure the books revealed nothing that would have startled the Cro-Magnon.

We had picked the fruit of one of four species of plants named strawberry, only two of which are edible. This one is called common strawberry in the "Peterson Field Guide to Wildflowers," wild strawberry in Lawrence Newcomb's "Wildflower Guide," and Fragaria virginiana in "Britton and Brown's Illustrated Flora."

The other strawberries are the wood strawberry, Fragaria vesca, which also are edible; the barren strawberry, *Waldsteinia fragarioides*, which is inedible; and the Indian strawberry, *Duchesnea indica*, which also is inedible.

Fragaria virginiana is the one that tastes really good. Common strawberries have three toothed leaflets (the five-leafleted cinquefoil is often mistaken for strawberry), and white, five-petaled flowers.

Common or wild strawberries most often grow in dry fields, frequently ones that are rocky, partially barren, or have been disturbed in the past few years. The plants spread by runners as well as by seed, so finding patches or clumps of strawberries is the rule, not the exception. Productive patches often can be found in the same area for several years, because the plant is a perennial.

The other edible wild strawberry may or may not be a native species, depending on who you believe. Newcomb calls the wood strawberry, *Fragaria vesca*, a native; Peterson's says it's an alien; and Britton and Brown calls it an alien over most of its range in North America but native northeastward. It is found in Europe, too.

Wood strawberry seeds grow right on the surface of the berry, whereas common or wild strawberries have their seeds recessed in pits or nodules on the surface.

The two other plants with strawberry in their names are from different genera and have yellow flowers instead of white. One, the barren strawberry, *Walsteinia fragaroides*, yields a dry, inedible fruit (hence its name). The other, Indian strawberry, *Duchesna indica*, makes a fruit that looks like a strawberry but does not

– Britton and Brown calls them "insipid."

Leave it to a naturalist to complicate a simple matter. Excuse me, I'm going out to pick some strawberries ...

Two feathers

One pink stick-on note in my mailbox at work caught my eye first. It floated attractively in a sea of other notes, memos, phone messages, and miscellany typically waiting for someone returning from vacation. I say attractively because it had two feathers taped to it, along with these words "Please identify."

That's easy, I thought. They're feathers. Next message, please.

After going through all my messages, I went back to the feathers. One of them I recognized right away as a tail feather from a downy woodpecker. It was about 2 inches long, black with white spotting down one edge. The feather was symmetrical, with a stiff shaft, indicating a tail feather. Had it been a wing feather, it would have been asymmetrical, with one side of the feather wider than the other.

(A digression, courtesy of my sons, who are dinosaur fans: The fossil remains of Archaeopteryx, which may or may not have been a descendant of dinosaurs and an early ancestor of birds, contain feather imprints which clearly indicate that the animal could fly. The wing feathers of Archaeopteryx are shaped identically to those of modern flying birds. Their asymmetrical shape would have had no value, and hence would not have evolved, unless they were used for flight.)

The other feather on the note stumped me at first. It was white, with wide-spaced orangy-brown bars on it. I could tell it was a body feather, probably from the chest, because the shaft and barbs felt relatively soft, and a bit of down clung to the base of the shaft.

Hmmm ... what has orange barring on the chest? Grouse? No. Turkey? No. It took me a while to clear the mental blockade the feather erected, but I finally remembered that several raptors have orange barring below in adult plumage. The most likely candidate found locally would be Cooper's hawk.

Birds "shed" their feathers – the right word is molt – pretty much the same way that cats and dogs shed their fur. Most songbirds go through a complete molt in the fall, and a partial molt in the spring. The spring molt involves only head and body feathers, usually bringing the bird into its colorful breeding plumage. So why did the downy woodpecker drop a tail feather in mid-July?

Suddenly it was clear that the two feathers taped to the note had an exciting story behind them. An adult Cooper's hawk, probably hunting for food for its nearly grown young, swept down on a feeding downy woodpecker, and snatched it with sharp talons. The woodpecker fought back, striking up at the hawk with its bill and dislodging a breast feather.

Perhaps the woodpecker even escaped, losing nothing but a tail feather, although this is unlikely. Adult Cooper's hawks are highly precise predators, and the two feathers probably are testimony to a successful hunt.

Star-nosed mole

Something scuffled in the leaves at the bottom of the window well near the front steps, making quite a ruckus. Window wells are very much like pit traps to small animals, which frequently fall in but cannot get out. Already this year I have rescued a baby rabbit and two or three toads from our window wells.

It is a good idea to prop a small, rough board in window wells, offering trapped animals a ramp to escape on before they starve or dehydrate.

Expecting another rabbit (because the rustling noise was a little too loud and persistent for a toad), I walked over and found instead a creature seldom encountered above ground. It was a star-nosed mole, and a good-sized one, too, stretching about 7 inches from its pink nose to the tip of its bristly tail.

The star-nosed mole is so-named because feelers ring its

fleshy pink nose, creating a star-like appearance. When the mole looks for food, the feelers move constantly.

Star-nosed moles, like their relative the eastern mole, live nearly all their lives below ground, and together the two are responsible for the networks of tunnels with raised roofs on lawns and in meadows. The feelers of the star-nosed are an adaptation to its existence in the dark underground, where the sense of touch gains superiority to sight or hearing.

By looking closely, I was just able to make out two dark spots on the star-nosed mole's head, where the eyes should have been. Moles can only perceive the presence or absence of light, and, like worms, usually react by moving away from light. I could see no sign of ears on the mole, although small ear openings are supposed to be present.

Star-nosed moles have several other interesting adaptations to life underground. Their feet are huge and webbed, ideally suited to digging. In addition, a mole's hairs each taper at the base, allowing the hairs to tip in any direction. In other words, you can pet a mole backward without ruffling its fur. This allows moles to go both backward and forward in tightly enclosed spaces.

Moles dig for both shelter and food, which for them includes earthworms, insects, and grubs. Both species of mole occasionally go for a swim, pursuing small fish and aquatic insects. Gardeners sometimes blame moles for damage to roots and bulbs of their favorite plants. In fact, moles are almost wholly carnivorous, eating their weight in food every day and consuming numerous harmful insects. Mice and voles do sometimes enter mole tunnels, and these omnivores can do considerable damage to plants.

I found a box to capture the mole with and, after showing it to my children, released it in the orchard, where it soon burrowed under the grass and disappeared.

Salamanders

Is there anyone who has not, at one time or another in their lives, gone through the woods turning over rocks and logs looking for salamanders? Granted, relatively few adults indulge in this kind of activity, but kids gravitate to salamanders instinctively.

Flip over a log just about anywhere and red-backed salamanders wriggle for cover. Red-backeds are the most ubiquitous salamander in the Northeast. When I dumped the water from my kids' plastic sandbox yesterday, I exposed half a dozen red-backs, who apparently otherwise lived quite contentedly under their petroleum-based shelter.

This species is named for the broad reddish stripe running lengthwise down its back, but not all red-backed salamanders are red-backed. An equally common version of the same species is known as the "lead-backed" salamander. This color morph is uniformly dark gray. Both the red-backed and lead-backed morphs show salt-and-pepper markings on the underside, a good field mark for this confusing species.

Any kid can tell you that salamanders must stay moist. For red-backed salamanders, keeping moist is a very serious matter. The red-backed salamander is a member of the salamander family *Plethidontidae*. This family's most unique trait is that none of its species have lungs, an adaptation that certainly would not work well for humans. *Plethidontidae* salamanders must exchange carbon dioxide for oxygen through their moist skin. The moisture facilitates gas exchange, so if a red-backed salamander stays out in the sun, it will not so much dry out as suffocate.

A cousin of the red-backed salamander, known as the slimy salamander, takes keeping moist to an extreme. It secretes a very sticky substance to cover its skin. Last week I found a slimy salamander under a boulder at Point Mountain, and after picking it up had the privilege of wearing this sticky coating until it wore off, since soap and water were not very effective on it.

Salamanders are amphibians, and most species lay their eggs in water. The eggs hatch into gilled larvae, which later transform into lunged adults. Red-backed and slimy salamanders skip the aquatic stage, however. They lay eggs in small clusters under damp logs, in moss, or other moist locations. The young salamanders complete their development in the eggs, and hatch as small replicas of the adults.

Not all salamanders are as adaptable and common as the red-backed and slimy. Most species prefer healthy, mature woodlands, and because of their relatively porous skin can be adversely affected by pollution or insecticide spraying. Since salamanders also depend on downed trees for shelter, salvaging fallen trees for firewood removes important habitat.

For now, salamanders remain fairly common where there is suitable habitat. Let's hope many remain for our children's children to find under rocks and logs 100 years from now.

Turkey vultures

Were you to climb a certain rocky face of Musconetcong Mountain, you might, if you were lucky, see a turkey vulture flapping hard with its 6-foot wings as it tried to get its seemingly cumbersome body aloft.

If you were exceptionally lucky, you might look up from your search for a handhold on the rocks in time to see where the bird took off. And, if your luck held, along with your handholds, you might reach the spot and hear an abrasive "sssssshshshsh," and know that you had found the nest, and that a milk jug-sized ball of white animated fluff huddled inside.

David Womer of Bloomsbury and I were lucky last weekend, and indeed found the nest of a turkey vulture.

A vulture nest really is not a nest by conventional standards. These birds lay their eggs in remote caves, usually on rocky cliffs. Once in a while they might nest in an abandoned building, and long ago, when big trees abounded, they nested in hollow logs.

Vultures build no nest. The female vulture merely plops her two eggs down on the floor of the cave. She incubates the eggs for almost six weeks, which means our vulture laid eggs in late April or early May.

Taking turns with Dave's flashlight, we stared down into the cave at the downy young, hissing defiantly, but crouching facing away from us. Actually the young bird was kind of cute, compared to the adult.

Adult turkey vultures look pretty ghastly, with blackish-brown, often ragged plumage and a head covered with bare, wrinkled skin. Their bill is hooked, like that of other meat-eating birds, but it is longer and thinner. Vultures eat dead things. Their head is naked because feathers would quickly become drenched with blood and gore. Bare skin is easier to keep clean.

That is the turkey vulture on the ground. The bird in flight is another matter, a graceful master of updrafts and thermals, sailing high or low with nary a wing-beat. The vulture is a past master at conserving energy, which is important when you have to wait for something to die before you can eat.

Overhead, the vulture appears as a large, mostly dark bird with its wings held up in a slight "V" or dihedral. The rear half of the vulture's wing, where the flight feathers are, is paler than the rest of the underside.

Turkey vultures are very common in the Northeast, thanks largely to our abundant deer (and hence abundant roadkills). In winter, vultures form roosts, sometimes containing more than 100 birds.

A few black vultures, a species with a more southern range, appear regularly with their more northerly cousin the turkey vulture. The black vultures are smaller, and have whitish wing tips on an otherwise all-black plumage. Their wing beats are faster than those of the turkey vulture.

It has been shown that vultures find their "prey" through a combination of sight and scent. Vultures have sensitive noses, a rare trait in the bird world but one that makes sense when the bird's food is usually rotten.

So, if you are going to lay down out in the open, it might be a good idea to take a shower first.

Turtles or moths?

Which to write about, the Polyphemus moth or the snapping turtles? It is a tough decision.

One voice says, "Go with the turtles. People can't relate to moths."

"Like they can to snapping turtles?" retorts the second voice.

"Moths are inconsequential," argues the voice rooting on the turtle's behalf.

"Tell that to the moths. And I beg to differ, especially when you're talking about a moth as big as a bat."

"Snapping turtles are bigger."

"Not the ones you want to write about. They were just hatchlings about to be smooshed by a car when you found them."

"Look, pal, those turtles are going to grow into 40-pound monsters, and I hope one of them bites you in the leg some day."

"They're not going to get the chance, because we let them go."

"We did?"

"Yeah, well, him anyway, the guy at the typewriter talking to himself, he let them go."

WELL, let's get re-focused here. Snappers or moth? The pleasant thing about nature writing is that there is no shortage of material. This is also the unpleasant thing about nature writing.

So this morning I was all set to write about the immense Polyphemus moth that our house lights attracted last night, and then what happens but two hatchling snapping turtles wind up on the road in front of my car, looking like moving lumps of mud. Which merits more attention?

The Polyphemus is one of the giant silkworm moths, a family so named because its members are big and spin a cocoon from silk. The adult moths of this family are often drawn to street or house lights, clinging to screens or fluttering around the seemingly irresistible source of light.

We had the flood lights on for some night-time basketball when this particular Polyphemus flew in, first to the lights and then into the garage, where it landed on the floor. The kids were impressed; the yellowish moth had a wingspread of about 5 inches. The species is named after the one-eyed giant Polyphemus of Greek mythology, because it has eye-like spots on each hindwing.

The snapping turtles, all covered with mud, apparently had just emerged from the ground along the roadside, where the mother turtle must have buried her 20 or so eggs. The shells on the hatchlings still felt soft and pliable, flexing slightly when I held the turtles between my fingers.

I decided to show the turtles to the kids in the park system's summer program before I released them in a marsh near where I found them. That would give me some time to think about what to write about.

"Hey, maybe he could write a little about both the moth and the turtles," said one voice.

"I think that is what he is going to do."

Wild turkey

"Do you think it will live until tomorrow, Mrs. Freiday?" asked Jack, a friend of my sons who was at our house for a sleep-over when all this happened.

"I don't know, Jack," my wife replied. "It's been through a lot."

"It" was a young wild turkey that had the misfortune of being in our yard when my wife, brought the dogs outside to do their business. Our Lab puppy Star, came back inside with something in her mouth.

"All I could see was its legs," Cathy told me later. "I felt awful, but I couldn't yell at Star. After all, she is a bird dog."

Remarkably, when the puppy released the baby turkey, it sat upright, apparently unhurt by its Jonah-like experience.

The question was, what to do with it? Cathy was not even sure what kind of bird it was at first.

"I looked in the nestling book in the library, since you weren't home, and figured out that it was a baby turkey. Then I read in another book that turkeys are "precocial," and after I read what that meant, I decided we would watch the bird overnight and let it go in the morning."

Wild turkey young are indeed "precocial." The word comes from the same Latin root as the word precocious, and means they are capable of moving around soon after hatching. Precocial birds hatch with their eyes open and are covered with down, and leave their nest within one or two days.

There are different levels of precociality. The most precocial young live totally independently from their parents. This pattern of development is found only in the chicks of a group of birds called megapodes, which are not found in North America. The eggs of these birds incubate in huge piles of decaying vegetation, and when they hatch the young dig their way to the surface, already feathered and able to fly.

Turkeys are not precocial to the extent that megapodes are. When hatched, young turkeys follow their parents and are shown food, which the babies capture themselves. Since the turkey Star found had some adult feathers growing in amidst the downy ones, it almost certainly was old enough to find food for itself.

Its best chance for survival as a wild bird would probably come if it were released and left to fend for itself. Hopefully, it would link back up with its mother or another turkey family, which would give it a better chance to avoid predators. In wild turkeys, family groups and hens without young normally join together to form flocks in summer, so this bird might find other turkeys and join the flock.

The next morning, the turkey awoke my wife, the kids and the dogs with its loud peeping. They (sans dogs) took the bird to the orchard and let it go. It immediately began walking about, catching insects, and peeping for company the whole time.

Garter snakes

As happens now and again if you aren't paying attention, while hiking recently I nearly stepped on a snake. I can't speak for the snake, but I was startled, to say the least.

It was a garter snake, the common local serpent with three yellowish stripes running lengthwise on its body. Perhaps eight out of 10 snakes found away from water in this area are garter snakes.

Garter snakes outnumber all other North American snakes, and have the largest range. Garter snakes live above the Arctic Circle in Canada, and all the way down in Mexico.

The garter snake has one close relative that may be found locally. This is the eastern ribbon snake. Ribbon snakes are much less common, and can be told by their more slender bodies, longer tails, and by the fact that their side stripes are farther up on their bodies. Ribbon snakes are very active and semi-aquatic, seldom found far from water.

This garter snake was a young one, only about 10 inches long. Its mother most likely gave birth last summer or early fall. Most snakes lay eggs, but garters have live young.

I was tempted to pick up the young snake, but prior experience with garter snakes caused me to observe it where it was instead. Garter snakes are not poisonous, although, like all snakes, they bite if harassed. Garter snakes gently nip, hardly denting the skin. Biting was not a problem, but this species, along with several other snakes, has an additional means of defense.

Many children can tell of the "garden" snake that "went to the bathroom on them." A captured garter snake often exudes an awful smelling liquid from its cloaca while wrapping and rewrapping itself on its captor to smear the goo all over.

This stinky habit is a predator defense mechanism. Lots of furred or feathered predators hunt snakes – predators ranging from red-tailed hawks to minks to bears. Smelling bad is a really good characteristic to have if something wants to eat you.

Another reason not to pick up a snake is that, even if it will not hurt you, you could easily hurt it. Like all creatures, snakes play an important role in nature, and are best left to go about their business.

This particular snake basked in the morning sun, most likely warming up in preparation for a hunting trip. Food for a snake this size means insects and especially earthworms, which garter snakes locate adeptly. Garter snakes are able to detect earthworms by scent, even underground.

As garter snakes grow older and bigger, they begin eating slightly larger animals, although because they are nonpoisonous and do not constrict their prey, the snakes limit their choice of food to mouse-sized or smaller. Toads, frogs, and occasional baby birds are prime fodder for adult garter snakes, which may reach 3 feet or more. A length of 18 to 24 inches is more typical for adult garter snakes.

After a time, I left the snake to its basking and continued down the trail. There is a fair chance I will encounter the same snake on the same trail again another time. The snake will remain in the same area for its six- to eight-year life span, if it is lucky enough to avoid its many predators.

Alive

Floating gently down the western horizon, the sun's mood changed as a river's does late in its course. Dominant and irresistible, at the height of its power just moments before, a river at its mouth suddenly meets an entity hopelessly more powerful than its own flow had ever been.

This summer sun, were it alive, would know night to be close at hand. And, although it flared red as it kissed the horizon, the final rays cast were soft and colored, mellow and quiet. Something more powerful than it was coming.

A shadow ascended a weathered gray post where the end of the river met the edge of the bay. The post, once part of a dock now long forgotten, seemed to cling to its vertical stance though the cedar it came from was 50 years dead. In not many years, the Atlantic tide and current would carry the post to some fisherman's outboard propeller, or to some teen-ager's beach fire.

The line between light and dark neared, and finally reached the round, flat top of the gray post. A bird stood on top of the post, feeling the line between light and dark rise through her body, feeling the cool on her legs and the warmth on her breast.

The sun's altered mood was not lost on the bird as she stood in the red rays in the cool of the June evening. The bird was tired. She had remained on that post since the sun's zenith, leaving only occasionally to fly a quavering circle over her nest. And over the intruder.

The bird had never seen an intruder like this, this close. These were always at a distance, far below as she flew or far away on the beach on the main island. This intruder stood erect, stood as her post seemed to want to do. It moved strangely along the shore, stopping to swing a long, shiny thing which then made clicking noises. If she could have thought about it, she would have realized the intruder was feeding along the shoreline just as so many of the other marsh creatures did. She did not think about it. The intruder fed very near her nest.

She had circled the intruder and called once or twice every few minutes for the past six hours. She did this because this was what she did.

She did not feed, because it did not matter.

She knew the intruder was more powerful than she.

The bird's eyes closed as she listened to evening sounds on the marsh; the intruder was gone. She knew without watching that the night herons had left their rookery and were on their way to share her feeding ground, but not her prey. She knew without prior arrangements that her mate fed on the sand bar and would until the sinking sun told him to return to warm the eggs, while she fed.

She knew without a tide table that the neap tide gently rose but would not reach the high water mark, that the moon was new, that the evening star would soon blink near the horizon. She knew the ospreys on the nearby tower did not eat birds. She knew, without knowing.

She knew, most of all, that the intruder had not found her eggs – and that, if it had, there was no time to begin another clutch.

She may even have known that she would not be back next year to try another time to replace her now 6-year-old body with a new one raised from a nest.

Men called this kind of bird a willet, for the sound they believed they heard in the bird's frantic calling. Men had no idea what the bird was.

She had returned to this marsh edge for five years now. She succeeded this year in completing her clutch of four eggs before a high tide flooded the nest or a gull or fox destroyed it. The eggs were now near hatching. She had never seen a chick of her own before.

The bird heard a call out on the marsh, a call moving closer, a call repeated over and over again. She opened her eyes, turning her head slightly as the image of a flying bird became the image of another like her and then became her mate. She knew her mate by the sound of the call, but at this moment, as the sun's final rays shrank to the horizon, at this moment she watched him return.

Her mate circled her post twice, flying on quavering wings, flashing the white in his wings, calling. He did not land next to her, though there was room on the post. He did not fly very near her. He flew to the nest, and settled on the eggs.

She lifted her wings and held them over her back an instant, saying silently in that instant: "willet."

Then she dropped off her post and winged towards the half-covered mud flat, calling as she went, the post in the rear of her eyes disappearing into the night. She crossed the river and the darkness and a stretch of salt hay, and then landed heavily (for she was a large bird, and tired) onto a mudflat already occupied by night herons and by a smattering of crippled or immature sandpipers lacking the strength or will to journey to their Arctic nesting places, as well as a few whose tundra nests had already failed and who were now 11 months and thousands of miles away from their next chance.

The bird quickly claimed her select feeding territory. She fed immediately, ignoring for the time being birds mistakenly crossing into her chosen ground as she searched for the life in the mud. She was tired and hungry from her day on the post.

In not many years, the tides and current would carry the post to some fisherman's outboard propeller, or to some teen-ager's beach fire. This bird would not be alive to see that happen, would not be alive to find another place to perch as she watched for intruders or her mate.

Perhaps one of the lives in the eggs in her nest would.

Cliff swallows

Most kinds of birds have finished nesting by late August and the woods no longer ring with song. I was surprised this past weekend to find cliff swallows still busily feeding young. The swallows are easy to recognize, with their blue-black backs, and tan rumps and foreheads.

Like many other birds, the cliff swallows soon will be departing for their wintering grounds. Cliff swallows, however, have a longer trip than most species. Some of them will winter as far south as Argentina, which means they fly 6,000 or more miles twice a year, just in migration. Since swallows feed on the wing, catching flying insects, they spend most of their year in the air. A typical cliff swallow probably flies more miles a year than an average person drives in five.

Like their close relative, the barn swallow, cliff swallows build mud nests on the sides of buildings and underneath bridges.

The birds I observed nest underneath a foot bridge crossing the Delaware River, and give a great show to observers on the bridge as they fly underneath. The cliff swallow's nest is unique, because when finished it is almost completely enclosed, with only a small opening for the birds to enter and exit through. This carefully constructed nest actually creates problems for cliff swallows, thanks to a troublesome bird imported from England.

The problem bird is the house sparrow. Humans brought house sparrows to this country in the mid-19th century, and the species is now very common around farms and in cities and towns.

House sparrows nest in cavities, and find the cliff swallow nests ideal homes. House sparrows frequently usurp cliff swallow nests, leaving the swallows out in the cold. The sparrows create such problems with the cliff swallows that the swallows are now a New Jersey threatened species.

Cliff swallows thrive under most of the Delaware River bridges, however, for a simple reason. House sparrows apparently do not like to nest over water, and so do not bother nests under bridges.

Since the Delaware is at its late summer lowest, I could walk under the foot bridge at Bull's Island and watch the cliff swallows bring food to their young. Cliff swallows sometimes forage quite a distance from their nests, and locate good feeding areas in an interesting way. If a bird makes a foraging trip but is unsuccessful, it will linger near the colony and wait for a successful bird to return. When the successful bird feeds its young and leaves, the unsuccessful bird will follow it to the food.

Cliff swallows depend on insects for food, and so leave the temperate region before frosts eliminate the insects. They will not return to New Jersey until April. Although these are the same birds that are famous for returning to California's San Juan Capistrano on the same day every year, in this region they are not quite as consistent. They will arrive sometime in April, returning whenever the weather suits them.

Touch-me-not

In nearly every ditch or wet meadow and along nearly every stream, spotted touch-me-not is blooming. Orange flowers with red spots identify this plant, a favorite of naturalists everywhere. The flowers have an unusual shape, being cup-like with a thin tube for nectar at the bottom.

Spotted touch-me-not, also known as jewelweed, is both useful and fun. Many know the plant for its ability to help cure poison ivy. The juice of the plant contains substances that reduce the itchiness and swelling caused by poison ivy. To treat poison ivy with jewelweed, merely crush the thick, succulent stems of the plant and rub the juice on affected areas.

I have had mixed results on poison ivy when I've treated it with jewelweed. Most of the time the treatment reduces the itchiness and rash, but the symptoms disappear within a few hours and occasionally the jewelweed seems to have no effect. Most people report similar results.

On a recent canoe camping trip, I used spotted touch-me-not to treat a severe case of sunburn, mostly because that was the only medicine available at the time. I should have known enough to wear sun screen on the water, but I didn't, and by evening my face was beet red, much to the delight of the teen-agers I was leading. I found some touch-me-not on the river-bank, and coated my face with the juice. The next morning my face felt cool and looked much less red, and the skin did not peel.

Touch-me-not or jewelweed grows abundantly nearly any-where the ground is moist, often forming a dense mat of vege-tation up to 5 feet high. It is hard to believe that this plant is an annual, and that all that vegetation dies back and disappears over the winter. Because the plant is so common, you needn't feel guilty about picking some. However, although the flowers are quite lovely, the plant wilts almost immediately after being picked, so jewelweed is a poor choice for bouquets.

Touch-me-not gets its name from its seed pods, which look like miniature pea-pods, about one-half to 1 inch long. When ripe, the pods literally explode at the slightest touch, sending the greenish seeds flying up to four feet. This is how touch-me-not disperses its seeds. A pod exploded in a closed hand reveals that the sides of the pod are coiled up like springs. Seeds can also be collected this way. The seeds are a surprise all their own, a wonderful pearly blue underneath their greenish overcoat. I have watched children spend up to a half-hour in a patch of touch-me-not, giggling with surprise every time a touched pod explodes.

Touch-me-not's alternate name, jewelweed, refers to the way dew collects in tiny beads on this plant's leaves, shining like jewels in the morning sun. Even more amazing is what happens to a jewelweed leaf held under water. Tiny hairs on the surface of the leaf trap a layer of air there, causing the leaf to turn silver under water. When the leaf is taken out of the water, it is still dry.

Katydid (and didn't)

We spent lunch watching a large green bug. It wasn't the most appetizing subject for eating entertainment, but the teenagers I was leading were unfazed. They took turns holding the insect, allowing it to climb on their arms.

The 2-inches-plus bug was a katydid, one of my favorite insects – and one of the most conspicuous August insects. You don't see katydids very often, but stand on your porch any August night and you will definitely hear them. A friend from Alexandria Township describes the katydids in his woods as "deafening."

Katydids are a startlingly green relative to the grasshopper, so green that they blend beautifully with the foliage of most deciduous trees. For some reason, the katydid we found walked across a brown patch of earth, making it very easy to spot.

The camouflage of katydids is enhanced by the fact that their wings, held tent-like over their backs, actually have a vein-like pattern similar to that found on many leaves. All species of katydids (there are actually several species) have very long antennae, which, though wispy, often exceed the length of their bodies.

The katydid's call is a raspy series of buzzy notes, roughly translated as "kate-ee-did," or "ehh-ehh-ehh" for the unimaginative. Katydids sometimes vary the number of syllables in their calls, so you get "kate did," "katy didn't," "katy sure didn't," and "katy surely didn't."

In some species, both male and female make noises; in others, only the male calls. The calling, like bird song, helps the sexes find each other and may also help katydids establish territories.

Like all insects, katydids are cold-blooded, and the rate at which they call so closely corresponds to the air temperature that there is actually a formula to figure degrees Fahrenheit based on katydid calls per minute. To some extent, katydids control their body temperature by behavior, moving to warmer areas when they are chilled and to cooler, shady areas when they begin to overheat.

We considered keeping our katydid as a group mascot, but decided not to. The katydid might not like the temperature ranges we chose, and would have a hard time finding its diet of leaves if forced to ride around on someone's shoulder.

Choruses of katydids call in or near mature trees. They normally call at night, although once in a while one will get going during the day, adding a little character to the monotonous droning of the cicadas, another grasshopper relative.

My dad always said that when the first katydid called, frost was due in six weeks. I heard my first katydid of the summer in mid-July, which means frost by Labor Day. Who knows?

Young foxes

A half-grown red fox bounded through the headlights and, with a touch of awkwardness, climbed the steep grassy bank edging the road.

Adult foxes travel with sinewy grace, but the young kits that over the next few weeks will make their first extended forays through their parents' range are still learning how to move like a fox. Unfortunately, many will become road casualties before they do.

The fox in my headlights survived this road crossing, white-tipped tail disappearing over the lip of the road. He or she was probably about 4 months old, and likely returned to its den well before morning. Red foxes often den in old woodchuck burrows, repaired and expanded to suit their new owners.

The happiest foxes this summer call a well-drained hillside home. Repeated rainstorms have made bathtubs of some of the lowland burrows. Since red foxes frequently move their kits from one den to another, even those that started a family on low ground no doubt are higher and drier now.

As summer progresses, the young foxes will learn from their parents, and on their own, how to be foxes: how to hunt, how to hide, how to move like a fox. We will see them more and more, foolish, gangly teen-aged foxes dashing across roads or pouncing awkwardly on grasshoppers in August meadows. Adult foxes do not like to be seen, but young foxes either do not know they should move in hiding or at night, or do not care. It should not be assumed, therefore, that there is something wrong with a fox abroad in summer daylight – that it is sick with rabies or distemper – any more than there is something wrong with a teen-ager who stays out until 3 a.m.

Foxes often bark on summer nights, a sound hard to describe but unmistakable once heard. Fox barks sound like a cross between a yowl and a scream, although the summer barks seem to agonize less than those of the winter breeding time. In summer, parent foxes bark often while teaching their young to hunt.

By September, the young hunt, hide and travel on their own. In late September or October, most disperse, seeking new home ranges miles from their natal area. This early fall dispersal is timed to coincide with the greatest possible abundance of fox food. Fall foxes stalk the summer's litters of rabbits, meadow voles, and squirrels, and pursue grasshoppers and other insects numbed by the early morning dew.

Even if a young fox fails to find animal food, vegetable food is available in abundance. Foxes will eat fruits of all kinds, and many nuts and seeds, so a young fox need not go hungry.

Snakes in the basement

"We're up to sixteen now," my wife said as I walked in the door the other night.

"How many did we have last year, again?" My memory isn't much for detail.

"Thirty-eight, not counting the big ones."

"Slow year, I guess."

Like more than a few country folk, we have milk snakes living around, and sometimes in, our house. These snakes love to hang around buildings with stone foundations. We began discovering our snakes the first fall we lived in this farmhouse.

Milk snakes are so-named because, long ago, country folk believed the snakes sucked milk out of cows. Of course, milk snakes are not at all interested in milk. They hide in the shelter of nooks and crannies in buildings, and hunt small animals, especially mice, which they kill by constricting.

Milk snakes are not poisonous. If you can put aside fears and superstitions, milk snakes are nice to have around.

In September, I receive many phone calls from people who see snakes in their homes, especially young snakes. Baby snakes in a house in August or September are almost invariably recently hatched m i l k snakes. T h e s e  snakes lay their eggs in crevices or cavities, sometimes with two or more snakes using the same place year after year. Cracks in basement walls are probably considered prime egg-laying sites. Each snake will normally lay about 15 eggs, so at least two females laid the eggs that resulted in our 38 serpentine visitors. The newly hatched snakes feed on insects and other invertebrates, although some probably will not eat until they emerge from hibernation next spring.

If adult snakes, meaning individuals more than 16 inches long, appear around the house in September, chances are good they intend to hibernate somewhere nearby, perhaps next to your foundation or in your basement. This is not such a bad thing, because milk snakes do eat mice, and they can get at them inside of walls and other place where cats cannot go.

Of course, it can be a bit disconcerting if you are doing laundry in the basement, as my wife was one day last spring, and a 2-foot snake slithers out of an armful of clothes.

Waiting for hawks

I need to see some hawks.

It's not that I haven't seen any lately, just that I haven't seen very many. During the summer breeding season, hawks of all kinds tend to be more secretive than at other times of year, and too busy, besides hunting food for their young, to do much soaring about where they can be observed.

At least red-tailed hawks are visible almost every day as they soar over the fields and roads in their search for rabbits and mice. Now and then a Cooper's hawk will flash across a clearing in pursuit of a jay or other songbird.

Another of the most visible summer raptors in our area is the American kestrel, a small, colorful falcon that prefers farm country. These birds often perch on telephone wires along the roads, where they can watch for their favorite summer prey, large insects.

A few weeks ago a northern goshawk flashed in front of my truck as I drove along the Musconetcong River in Bethlehem

Township. I was surprised to say the least, since goshawks are locally quite rare as nesting birds.

Except for chance sightings like this, the best time to see all raptors, from kestrels to eagles, is during their fall migration, when hundreds of hawks, eagles and falcons might pass a watch during a single day. If you have never done it, don't start hawk-watching unless you and your family are prepared to handle an addiction that lasts three months every year.

Hawk-watching begins in earnest in September, when broad-winged hawks begin the journey to their wintering grounds in Central and South America. I have seen more than 1,000 broad-wings together at one time in mid-September, circling in what hawk-watchers call a "kettle." The best chance for seeing kettles like this comes at any of the well-known hawk-watching look-outs.

People flock to lookouts from September right through to the end of November, when the last red-tailed hawks, goshawks and eagles pass by on their journeys to points south.

It is troubling that my home county of Hunterdon has no well-known hawk watching spot. The nearest good places are Chimney Rock in Somerset County and Scott's Mountain in Warren County. Further north in the state, people watch from Raccoon Ridge and Sunrise Mountain, both on the Kittatiny Ridge. The famous Hawk Mountain in Pennsylvania is farther southwest along the same ridge.

Inland hawk-watching hot spots are always associated with a ridge, usually one running in a northeast to southwest direction. After an autumn cold front passes, northwest winds running along these ridges create strong updrafts, which hawks ride to conserve energy. Ridge lines may also serve as directional guides to migrating hawks.

Two major northeast-southwest ridgelines cross Hunterdon County. To the north, Musconetcong Mountain, the southern-most part of the New Jersey Highlands, certainly looks like it should have hawk-flight potential. To the south, the long, low

Sourland Mountain definitely supports a small but little-studied hawk flight.

We'll have to wait until September to really explore these areas – and I, for one, can hardly wait.

Apple orchards

Apple orchards are great places for wildlife, which also makes them great places to observe wildlife. Even a single apple tree draws wildlife in excess of most other tree species. This is never more true than in late summer and fall, when most animals prepare for winter either by collecting and storing food or by eating large amounts of food, which will be converted to layers of fat stored for the cold months ahead.

Since fall songbird migration is under way in earnest, now is a good time for birders to search out orchards that receive early-morning sunshine. Sunlit edges attract insect-eating birds, because on chilly mornings most insect activity concentrates here.

Unsprayed orchards are usually full of insect activity, and dozens of different birds prey on these insects. A quick scan of a bird checklist reveals that I have seen about 100 species in orchards over the past few years, including nearly all of the brightly colored wood warblers (which are almost totally insectivorous). Game birds such as ruffed grouse and wild turkeys also forage in orchards, eating both ground-dwelling insects like grasshoppers and fallen fruit.

Apples in untended orchards fall in droves in September, and several kinds of mammals are drawn to such places to feed. White-tailed deer are well known for their fondness for apples, but the list of diners at the orchard will also include woodchucks, gray squirrels, red squirrels, chipmunks and cottontail rabbits. The rabbits prefer the grass and forbs growing under the trees, rather than the apples.

At night, a different set of creatures might come for a midnight snack, including opossums, skunks, raccoons, black bears, and even foxes. Red and gray foxes are primarily carnivorous, but a small but consistent portion of each species' diet will include fleshy fruits and seeds. In summer and fall, this portion of their diet may account for 25 percent of the calories they take in. Of course, orchards are prime places for the carnivores to hunt, since mice and other small rodents find such places attractive. Apple orchards, especially those that are not severely pruned, also provide excellent cover for wildlife. Unchecked, the trees form dense clusters of branches, which make excellent hiding places for birds. Many older apple trees will be partially hollow. If the cavities are large enough, they might become dens for squirrels, raccoons or opossums. Trees with cavities at the base might be used by skunks or even a sleepy gray fox.

Higher up, holes made by woodpeckers or left when a branch has broken off will be used for nesting and roosting by chickadees, titmice, great-crested flycatchers, white-breasted nuthatches and screech owls. It is a good idea to check orchards for such holes, which, if you are lucky, might provide a rare daytime look at a sleeping screech owl.

For all these creatures, apple orchards are like a quality bed-and-breakfast inn, offering a comfortable place to sleep, and plenty to eat when they wake up.

The bobolink's call

"You're my chair, Daddy."

"I thought I was your Daddy, daughter."

"Well, you are, but except sometimes you're all snugly," she says, squirming side to side in my arms to prove it. We are sitting on the back steps on a chilly late-August morning, watching summer midwife the birth of autumn. The cement steps are quite cold on my bare feet; Rebecca has her feet planted firmly and flatly against my legs.

A loose flock of small birds, golden yellow in the low light of sunrise, comes out of the north, from the direction of Cushetunk Mountain, which, although 10 miles away, is crisply outlined in the clear air just arrived from Canada. The birds are calling; the sound resembles a somewhat metallic rendition of the word "boink," repeated over and over again. The sound and the rich, yellowish, straw-like color of the birds identify them as southbound bobolinks.

Bobolinks nest in weedy hayfields and damp meadows across the northern half of the United States. Their numbers have declined in the East, likely from progressively earlier cuttings of hayfields. Because these birds nest on the ground, they are vulnerable to mowing, as well as predators like cats. They have become scarce enough that in New Jersey they are considered a threatened species, although they are not that uncommon where the right habitat can be found.

"Do you hear those birds, Rebecca? The ones overhead that sound like they're saying `boink, boink?'|"

Rebecca is 6, and still knows how to listen. She is still as stone in my lap, her head cocked to catch the sound. She reminds me of her 6-month-old puppy. When I reach for my cup of coffee, steaming in its ceramic mug beside us on the steps, she softly admonishes, "Shhhh." We are quiet together for a moment.

"I hear them, Daddy."

The bobolinks pass over the house, a shimmering wave of 20 autumn-blown leaves that disappear behind the roof-line, going south. We can hear their wings and their calls, and I at least can hear their message. Sipping coffee, I wonder if Rebecca can, too.

"Those are bobolinks. I always listen for them around now. They tell when fall is coming. They live way down in South America all winter, and come up around here to have their babies. Now they are going back south again."

"Maybe we can put some birdseed out for them, if we have any." Becka turns her eyes from over us back toward Cushetunk as she speaks, and also says, "I just heard a frog jump into the pond. Maybe he will go in the leaves and mud because it is cold." Rebecca shivers and says, "Can you put a fire in the fire-place?"

She knows how to listen, and she hears the bobolink's call very well.

Fall

Broad winged hawk

Fall

Screech owls

Yesterday afternoon I was confronted with an important decision: mow the lawn or repair the screech owl nest box? Which would be the more meaningful activity in the great scheme of things?

I pulled the hammer from my tool box and dragged the ladder out to the orchard.

The box will not be used for nesting until next spring, but hopefully a screech owl will adopt it as his or her winter quarters. It will provide a safe and snug repose, placed 20 feet high, facing south, and lined with pine have shavings. Why, if I could fit, I'd crawl right in. Since I can't, there is no bird I'd rather enjoy the box than a screech owl.

The screech owl is my favorite bird, for a variety of reasons. The species certainly is not rare or endangered. Screech owls hunt and roost all over eastern North America, and can be remarkably abundant for a raptor. Raptors, perched as they are at the top of the food chain, tend to be the least abundant type of bird.

For the Christmas Bird Count in Hunterdon County, my nocturnal friends and I have no trouble at all calling in 20 or more screech owls in a relatively small area. If we cover 5 percent of the county (and I doubt we do), that means at least 400 screech owls terrorize the mice between Point Mountain and the Sourlands. I'd bet there is a screech owl within a quarter-mile of most readers right now.

Screech owls fascinate me in part because they are beautiful, garbed in bright red-brown in the red phase or a more cryptic bark color in the gray phase. The birds' eyes glow bright yellow, appearing severe when the birds are angry or threatened, but sometimes giving a comical expression to the owner's face. One of the "eared" owls, screech owls sport two prominent feather tufts at the top of the head, which can be raised or flattened depending on the bird's mood.

The best thing about screech owls is that they come when I call, responding about as reliably as my dog (meaning usually, but not always). The call of a screech owl is an easily imitated, whinnying whistle that means either "come here, sweetie" or "this is my territory, punk," depending on the cadence and the pitch. Hats have been knocked off heads by aggressive or love-torn screech owls responding to human impostors.

By the time my owl box was repaired and secured in the tall ash next to the orchard, darkness had arrived. I whistled an invitation for a few minutes, just for luck, just to let the owls know the welcome mat was in place.

Perhaps today one of the little owls will be at the opening of the box, basking in the warmth of the rising sun. I think I'll get my coat and see.

Travels of a thrush

A typically gory Adirondack sunset spattered like pizza pie all across the western horizon above Fish Creek Camp, near Saranac Lake, N.Y. At first, I had little enthusiasm for the scene – we had just finished the second leg of a 90-mile canoe race, and I hurt in places that before today I didn't know I had.

But then a loon called out on the lake, with that low tremolo you always hear on Canadian tourism commercials, and the scene came to life.

A soft, musical note, obviously from a small bird but sounding like a spring peeper, dropped down from the sky overhead, and I looked up in time to see a thrush leave the trees and begin to gain altitude as it headed south. It was little more than a silhouette, but the call matched one the Swainson's thrush often gives. Like almost all songbirds, Swainson's thrushes migrate at night, and this one might reach the New Jersey state line by dawn if the wind stayed favorable.

We finished the race the next day, near Lake Placid, and after watching the remaining canoes come in behind us we loaded up and headed for the New York Thruway. I drove, and had long forgotten the thrush.

We took a break near dark at the last rest stop on the Thruway. While my partners went into McDonalds, I stood by the car looking up at the sky and listening for whatever might be heard over the roar of the traffic. A call floated down again, that same soft note, and I wondered if the Swainson's thrush that called near Saranac had rested for the day in the woods behind the rest stop, feeding up on insects gleaned from the low foliage and leaf litter before heading south once more. It had a ways to go, because these birds spend their winters no nearer than southern Mexico, and sometimes as far south as Argentina.

I was home in Hunterdon at 11 p.m. After enduring the ravaging greeting of a chocolate Lab to whom a three-day absence was the same as a stint in the Army, I unloaded my gear and found some leftovers in the fridge. The dog joined me on the back steps for dinner – you never need to ask a Lab if it wants a little snack.

The quiet blew like a breath of clean air after the roar of the highway. A few katydids called – very slowly, as if they were stiff with the cold. Otherwise the surroundings were silent, which was fine with me, and the stars bright enough to reveal the dark mass of Cushetunk Mountain about 15 miles to the north.

My hand was reaching for the door knob when I noticed the dog, facing north and standing quite still, with her ears forward, listening. I listened, too, and heard one more time a soft note in the sky that meant a bird traveling south, my bird I fancied, heading toward its winter home.

I was already home, and since I knew how the traveler up above must feel, I silently wished it well.

The broad-winged blues

You would think that a flight of 8,000 broad-winged hawks would carry some sort of a message, but there doesn't seem to be a message there right now.

Maybe it's because watching is just fun, not particularly poignant. Maybe the message would be there, the story clearer, if the broad-wingeds swirling 3,000 feet overhead wrote it, instead of some dumb observer, binoculars in one hand and can of iced tea in the other. For the broad-wingeds, after all, migration is about life and death. Humans can watch it all on TV.

Or maybe not. Hawk-watching is not just watching, not for hawk-watchers. The broad-wingeds draw our hearts to them as they kettle, glide and soar over the ridges. They are as essential to our existence as clothes, or food, or air, as essential as forest, ridges and sun are to the broad-wingeds.

We need to see those birds, and we feel pain if we cannot.

The pain for me started Friday, Sept. 10. I had the day off, had taken it off intentionally to watch hawks. Chris, the official hawk counter at the Chimney Rock lookout, asked me to cover the watch for the day, which is like asking a broad-winged hawk if it wants to fly south in September.

Rainy and unsettled weather crumpled the flight that Friday, which did not particularly bother me. Forty-five hawks passed, including 24 ospreys, which tend to ignore the weather.

I was content with the flight, but felt almost afraid as I left the lookout that night. The little black calendar that runs my life said it would be Tuesday, Sept. 21, 11 days away, before I would be free to watch hawks again.

I knew, Chris knew, anyone who knows anything knew the big flight would happen before Sept. 21, and there was not a damn thing I could do about it.

A cold front passed the night after my watch, bringing impressive northwest winds as the air cooled and the sky cleared. The shutters tapped a hard beat on the walls and the screens hummed along when the front came through. Imagining a bird aloft in that kind of wind, I felt a sliver of hope. Maybe the wind will be too strong tomorrow. Broad-wingeds like still air, which allows thermals to form. Thermals, rising bubbles of warmed air, make or break a broad-winged flight. High winds simply blow the rising currents apart.

Strong winds did keep the flight grounded on Saturday, Sept. 11, at least until late afternoon. Chris called that night to tell me they had recorded 140 broad-wingeds at Chimney Rock, all after 2:30 in the afternoon. The little black calendar said one day down, 10 days to go.

All the hawk-watch regulars were expecting a big flight the next day, Sunday, Sept. 12. Conditions were going to be perfect: a recent front, clear skies and light winds, and the date matched the big flight date from last year. It seemed inevitable.

If a man could only control the weather ...

I could not control the weather, but whatever power does acted on my behalf that Sunday. The day started well at Chimney Rock, but a miracle high-pressure cell moved in from the Southwest and crushed the flight before it really got going. Two days down, nine days to go.

Not a chance in the world, Don. You're going to miss the flight. The problem, the real problem here, is that just like a lot of other people you've gotten so locked into a schedule designed to make yourself some sort of a professional success that you don't have time to do what's really important to you.

Which means that you better change the way you measure success.

The high-pressure cell, with its Southwest winds, held its ground Monday, Tuesday and Wednesday. The temperature spiked remarkably, reaching 93 degrees on Wednesday, when only six raptors of any kind passed Chimney Rock.

Days like that Wednesday may be what makes the big days so important. I can't say I was glad to be working instead of watching, but hawk-less skies can get to you. You stand there scanning, scanning, scanning, until high noon passes and your last iced tea is history and the arms holding the binoculars wilt like undernourished roses.

Happiness cannot be understood until sadness is also known. Thus sayeth hawk-watchers-turned-philosophers.

A new trace of hope crept into my heart on Thursday, when a new crummy-weather system arrived, bringing cloudy, rainy, misty, miserable weather. Clouds and rain stayed until Saturday night – can you believe it? I couldn't. Could this year's big day wait until next Tuesday?

The shaking of my house Saturday night answered the question in the negative. The front passed, and the weather band radio said clear skies by mid-morning Sunday, at the latest. Tens of thousands of broad-wingeds – not to mention kestrels, sharp-shinneds, eagles, merlins, peregrines, warblers, dragonflies, EVERYTHING – had been waiting for eight days now to head south. The first clear chance that came, they would take it. And I would be working.

On Sunday morning, Sept. 19, warblers chipped from every tree. The winds were still a little unsettled, but the insect-eating birds could not wait any longer and had made a flight after midnight. The day passed, and I knew I was missing it.

After work, my kids and I went visiting at my father's house. Dad lives on the second Watchung Mountain, quite close to Chimney Rock, and my ulterior motive was to catch the tail-end of the flight of the year.

Between 4 o'clock and 5 o'clock in the afternoon, I sat on the deck peering across the valley through my spotting scope. Raptors of all kinds were moving along the first Watchung, Chimney Rock's ridge. Here a kestrel, there a harrier, there a kettle of broad-wingeds; even an eagle. It wasn't exactly the best way to watch the flight, but at least I was seeing some of it.

We were cleaning up the dinner dishes when Timmy, playing out on the deck, called "Look, look, LOOK!" I rushed to the door.

Right over the house, a kettle of at least 300 broad-wingeds was breaking. The birds were settling into the trees for the night, like popcorn spilling from a bowl. The broad-wingeds would use our forest for only one night; by 9 a.m. tomorrow, they would be in the air again.

Another bird appeared overhead, a much bigger bird, a brown bird with flat wings and white mottling beneath. I called Dad, and through his picture window he watched the first bald eagle he had ever seen. It circled over the lawn before setting its wings and dropping into the woods.

Oh, well, at least I got a piece of the action. Which is a cheap, totally inadequate way of describing what I missed.

Then a thought crept through the disappointment. If all these birds pitched into the trees, that means tomorrow there will be another flight. The clear sky and pink sunset attested to that. In fact, tomorrow could be even a bigger day than today. Not that it matters; tomorrow is only Monday, and I can't get off until Tuesday. The thought left, quickly replaced by another.

When I talked to Chris that night, he described a record-breaking day for the watch, with 4,287 broad-wingeds and an unbelievable 18 bald eagles. I wondered aloud whether Monday was going to be even better. He wondered the same thing.

Sleeping is hard when you've got the broad-winged blues. I was going to miss two big flights, back to back. Something's wrong with this picture, I said to myself as I fell asleep.

I woke before dawn Monday, Sept. 20, 1993, feeling much better, and as I write these words I realize a message did fly with the 8,425 broad-wingeds migrating that day:

I took the day off to watch them.

Late bloomers

Spring traditionally is the favored time to go looking for wildflowers (or are we most eager to find something blooming then?) However, a number of unusual, beautiful, or just plain interesting wildflowers do not become conspicuous until autumn.

In woodlands throughout the area, the most obvious early autumn flower is white snakeroot (*Ageratina altissima*). Snakeroot reaches 4 feet in height, with white, fuzzy flowers in a broad, branching cluster at the top. White snakeroot is one of only a few common forest flowers that bloom in late summer and fall, a time when little light reaches the forest floor.

Two possible derivations of the name "snakeroot" have been suggested. One refers to snakeroot's long and twisty roots, a feature I have not really noticed when I've taken the time to uproot the plant. The other source of the name is said to be the highly poisonous nature of white snakeroot's roots. I have not been inclined to try to prove or disprove that one.

In a wet, open woodland I recently found some turtlehead (*Chelone glabra*) blooming. This snapdragon relative has opposite, toothed leaves and a very unusual white flower. The top lip of the flower arches over the lower lip to give the whole thing a striking resemblance to a turtle's head. The Latin word "chelone" in fact means "head of a turtle."

Turtlehead grows only in wet areas, usually in places that are at least dappled with sun. Butterfly enthusiasts should note that turtlehead is the only food plant used by the Baltimore check-erspot. This black-and-orange butterfly is very local in distribution, seldom found far from the wetlands that hold turtlehead plants for its larvae to feed on.

At this time of year, you hardly have to look past the roadside to find spotted knapweed (*Centaurea maculosa*) in bloom. Pinkish-purple flowers grace the 1- to 3-foot stems, making knapweed resemble thistle. The stems are not spiny, however, and have a characteristically gray-green color. Spotted knapweed is named for the black spots on the bracts covering the base of the flowerhead. The plant typically grows on disturbed ground – for example, virtually paving a gravelly abandoned airport runway near my home.

One of the latest-blooming flowers is the fringed gentian (*Gentiana crinita*). These stunning plants do not begin to open their flowers until October. Look for them along field edges and in moist meadows. The plant itself, at 1 to 3 feet, may be shorter than the grass surrounding it. Its flowers are a brilliant violet-blue, and each flower's four petals are fringed with long hairs.

Fringed gentians are the one of the most beautiful wildflowers in our area, providing a fitting finale to the flowering season.

In praise of ragweed

It has been a good year for ragweed, as recent record-breaking pollen counts indicate. Perhaps most people would refer to it as a bad year for ragweed instead.

While walking my kids out to the bus stop today, I noticed hundreds of ragweed plants lining the driveway and along the road. About a dozen goldfinches picked at the plants, as well as some house finches and the first white-throated sparrow of the fall.

Ragweed causes more sniffles, coughs and sinus problems than just about any other plant. In addition, it leaves much to be desired in the beauty department. Ragweed looks kind of scraggly, with a vaguely fern-like leaf and dozens of obscure, small green flowers per plant.

Few people have kind words for this plant, except those that know something of ragweed's value to wildlife. More than 75 kinds of wildlife feed on ragweed seeds, including some of our best known and loved birds. Goldfinches, white-throated and song sparrows, and dark-eyed juncoes (also called snowbirds) feed heavily on ragweed when it is available. Gamebirds such as doves, bobwhite quail, pheasants, and wild turkeys all love the seeds.

Ragweed has several attributes which make it desirable to wildlife. Each plant produces an enormous number of seeds, and the seeds themselves are rich in oil, providing a high-calorie meal for birds. Ragweed seeds persist on the plant well into winter. This means that the seeds are accessible to wildlife even when several inches of snow or ice coat the ground.

None of the 15 species of ragweed can be purchased from a greenhouse. I imagine you would get some pretty funny looks if you asked for it.

The most abundant species, common ragweed (*Ambrosia artemisiifolia*), is found in cultivated fields, along roadsides, in city lots, and just about anywhere else the ground has been disturbed. The plant often comes up in sidewalk cracks, and in border gardens. Construction sites are prime places for ragweed as well.

Ragweed is a pioneer invader of tilled or burned ground, and can be encouraged merely by turning the soil over. Because the ragweeds are annuals, perennials such as goldenrods, asters and little bluestem grass generally replace them in two to four years if the soil remains untilled.

In fact, a good landscaping technique for attracting wildlife is to annually till a few strips of earth, or a small field, and allow annual weeds to grow. This is most beneficial if done right alongside brushy areas or hedgerows, because that way species feeding on the annual plants have escape cover nearby.

Your human neighbors might not approve, but your wildlife neighbors certainly will.

Feeding the birds

White-throated sparrows and juncoes have returned after their breeding season in the northern forests. Right on schedule, the first individuals of both species appeared here during the last week of September. The return of these birds is the signal to set up your bird feeders.

If you feed the birds in winter, you might be interested in knowing that many of the whitethroats and juncoes (which are often called snow birds) are the same ones that were eating sunflower seeds at your feeder last year. Bird-banding studies show that white-throated sparrows will return year after year to the exact same bush where they spent their first winter.

Of course, many feeder birds spend the entire year in same area. Among these are the familiar chickadees, titmice, cardinals and woodpeckers. These species are non-migratory, a behavior pretty unusual in North American birds. More than 80 percent of the continent's birds migrate. Some move only a few miles, while others migrate thousands of miles every spring and fall.

People frequently ask, "How can I get more birds at my feeder?" or "What is the best kind of bird seed?" or "How can I attract cardinals?"

In this area, the best feeder set-ups should offer at least four different kinds of feed. The core of a feeding operation is a large tube- or house-type feeder filled with pure sunflower seeds. Either black oil or white-striped sunflower seeds work, although cardinals seem to prefer the larger striped seeds, while smaller birds like chickadees go for the oil type. Mixtures of the two types are available.

Another "must" for a feeding station is a seed mixture containing whole or cracked sunflower seeds, white millet, cracked corn, and peanuts. This mixture should be placed either on a tray-type feeder or scattered on the ground. Many birds, including cardinals, juncoes, and most sparrows, prefer to feed on a flat surface or the ground. Spreading seeds on the ground can increase the diversity of birds at a feeding station; in the right area, even pheasants and wild turkeys can be attracted.

A third type of food to offer is suet (beef fat). The simplest way to offer this high-energy food source is to fill a mesh onion bag and hang it from a tree limb. Another method is to attach chunks of suet to a tree trunk by nailing quarter-inch mesh screening over the suet. Suet appeals to woodpeckers, chickadees, titmice, nuthatches, and others.

The fourth basic food to offer at a bird-feeding station is thistle or niger seed. This very small seed is attractive primarily to finches, including goldfinches, purple finches and pine siskins. Thistle seed is expensive and requires a specially designed feeder with small holes, but seems to last a longer time than similar amounts of sunflowers.

The location of a feeding station is almost as important as what you feed there. The best sites offer protection from the wind and exposure to the morning sun. Some kind of shelter, such as shrubs, trees or tangled hedgerows, must be nearby to provide cover from inclement weather and predators.

Maintaining a continuous feeding station can be expensive; for example, I use about 80 pounds of sunflowers, 60 pounds of mixed seed, and 10 pounds of thistle per month from Oct. 1 to May 1, at a total cost of about $60 per month. However, the joy and satisfaction of watching dozens of birds thronging to a feeder on a wintry morning makes the expense very much worthwhile.

Hunter and the hunted

I left a message in case the editor of my column came hunting for me: "If Rick calls, tell him I am out gathering material to write about."

It was past the column's deadline, but a beautiful fall day beckoned.

"Tell him I'll get him something by tonight."

I went hunting myself, bow hunting for deer. I knew I'd find something to write about if I did, because something remarkable always unfolds when I wait silently for a deer, or ease carefully through the woods scouting for deer sign.

Dressed in quiet, camouflage clothes, attentive to where the wind takes their scent, hunters have the best chance to see wildlife close up.

I wasn't disappointed. At 3 o'clock in the afternoon, the sound of rushing wings and the excited chattering of gray squirrels announced the presence of a predator. I could hear the scrabbling of the squirrels' claws as they rushed to their treetop nests. Sure enough, a red-tailed hawk swept past, landing on a limb not 20 yards away. I'd swear the bird wore a chagrined look, as he glowered all around, looking for something small and furry for dinner.

Seeing a red-tailed hawk is always exciting, but certainly is not unusual. Red-tails are thriving, in spite of all the changes man has wrought to the landscape. Red-tailed hawks like roads. They like to hunt along highways, capturing rodents and snakes in the grassy median strips. They thrive in farm country, sitting in fencerow trees watching the ground below for a slight movement that means dinner. In winter, migrant red-tails concentrate near garbage dumps because of all the rats they can find there. Red-tails contrast with many other birds, which require forest or solitude, and so disappear in proximity to man.

I see red-tailed hawks almost every time I hunt, but this one lent some insight into the species' predatory abilities. After watching the hawk for a while, I turned my attention to some distant deer. Suddenly, quite close by, I heard what sounded like a child jumping up and down in a pile of dry leaves. I looked up to see the redtail perched on top of a squirrel nest, methodically ripping it apart with its talons. I wouldn't want to be that squirrel, I thought to myself.

The squirrel got the best of a bad situation. It waited in its

nest as long as it could. I'd like to think the squirrel calmly cal-
culated his odds, but more likely he huddled in his nest para-
lyzed by terror. I could see the red-tail's talons quite clearly from
15 yards, curving sharp claws about an inch long. I'll bet they
looked longer to the squirrel.

I couldn't see any way out for the squirrel, but the squirrel saw
it differently. He waited to make his move until the red-tail had
scattered most of the nest onto the forest floor.

Like a gray bullet, the rodent shot down out of the bottom of
the nest and ducked into a hole at the base of the tree trunk,
leaving the red-tail with only a fist full of leaves – and me with
a story to tell.

The gray squirrel's leap

A very loud "thunk" came from the woods road ahead of me,
as though something had fallen from the trees overhead.
Sounds of rapid scurrying in dry leaves followed the "thunk."

The low light of twilight, combined with the fact that my
eyes were fried from 10 hours of looking for hawks in an impos-
sibly blue sky, made it difficult to see what had happened in the
path ahead.

Something had struck the ground hard, that much was clear.
The sound resembled that of a punted football striking the turf
after soaring high over the stadium. Whatever hit the ground
was an animal, or at least it seemed so; it had to be, because it
scurried off the path.

What would be up in a tree in the woods, fall, but survive an
impact strong enough to knock a horse off its feet? The answer
was obviously a gray squirrel, although the animal's ability to
survive the impact made a cat a likely contender. Cats, after all,
have nine lives.

Looking overhead, it was clear that the squirrel had attempted a leap from the top of a 40-foot red oak on the right side of
the path to a slightly larger one on the left. Despite their wide-
spreading branches, at least 8 feet separated the two trees at the

closest point.

Perhaps the squirrel hurried since the sky had darkened rapidly, and darkness means danger to a gray squirrel. Perhaps an early-hunting great horned owl had soared over the oaks just as the squirrel attempted his jump, breaking its concentration. Perhaps the branch the squirrel used as a launching pad, dry from the drought, had broken as he jumped.

It could be that the squirrel carried one of the thousands of red oak acorns littering the forest floor this year, a bedtime snack that would be bitter for us but tastes just fine to squirrels.

Perhaps there are no excuses, and the squirrel had just screwed up his jump and fallen 40 feet as a reward for his effort.

Wild animals do make mistakes, but much less often than people do, for a simple reason: A mistake for a wild animal often results in death. Over the course of a species' evolution, the animals that make mistakes are weeded out, and the most perfect survive to pass their genes on to the next generation.

Somehow, this squirrel avoided the Grim Reaper, bouncing up from a long fall and hopping quickly off to his den tree. He will be sore in the morning, probably about the way I feel after playing "touch" football with my kids for an afternoon, but will be up and after those acorns once again.

From little acorns grow

I have been spreading good will, in the form of acorns. This job has traditionally been left to squirrels and blue jays, but where I live tradition needs a helping hand. Since people cut down the oak trees that grew on this small part of the Sourland Mountain, people ought to help put them back. Or so my thinking goes.

Acorns grow into a naturalist's dream: tall, thick oaks with spreading branches, sprinkled by oak flowers and colorful warblers in spring, and dropping a bounty of food for squirrels, deer, and wild turkeys in autumn. As the trees age, woodpeckers work over their dead limbs, and raccoons find homes in the hollow trunks.

Though many of the fields in my area are growing up with young trees, oak saplings are not among them. As abandoned fields revert to forest, the trees sprouting first are those with seeds that can travel.

Eastern red cedars and dogwoods grow berries, which are in turn eaten by birds. A bird's gut digests and absorbs the fruits from these trees, but the seeds pass through, dropping wherever the bird happens to be. Eastern red cedars and dogwoods find their way to an old field very quickly.

Maples, ashes, and tulip poplars produce light seeds, with wings attached, and only the weather limits the distance these seeds can go. Maples, ashes, and tulips also colonize old fields in short order.

But oaks? Acorns are usually chewed by the critters that eat them, and can not survive the trip through an animal's gut. Acorns are heavy, and drop straight from their parent trees. Oak trees need animals that pick up their acorns, carry them away, and then put them down or bury them without damage. Enter the blue jay, the squirrel – and me.

Jays do a fine job with the smaller species, the pin oaks and scarlet oaks, which make acorns small enough to fit in a beak. The oaks I want most, though, are the big ones, with big acorns: red oak, chestnut oak, white oak.

These big nuts are very popular with squirrels, and are buried throughout a squirrel's home range for later consumption. Here is the rub: squirrels only move about in the 5 or so acres they call home, seldom going farther. The oaks on the neighbor's property a half-mile away are going to take a whole bunch of years to make it as far as these overgrowing fields.

My family and I have a larger home range than a squirrel, and so last night got on our bikes and rode to a spot nearby where acorns rained down on the road. We collected a basketful, and carried them back to a place that has none. Some we tucked under the ground, some we just broadcast in the hope they would sprout.

Then we sat on the back steps and watched the sun set and I thought, if just one of those acorns sprouts and grows tall, we will have accomplished more than many.

Woolly bears

Folk-tale ways to predict just what kind of winter it's going to be abound, ranging from the amount of fat on the back of a deer to the thickness of a squirrel's tail. One of my favorite methods, just as accurate (or inaccurate) as the rest of them, is to examine the colors on woolly bear caterpillars.

There are two ways to check a woolly bear's forecast. One involves the total amount of black on the animal. The more black, the colder and harsher the winter will be. My son found a nearly all-black woolly bear last week. Guess I better split some more firewood.

The other interpretation of woolly bear forecasts is more detailed. The width of the black band at the front of the animal represents the length of autumn, while the black at the hind end tells how long the spring will be. The brown band in the middle represents the length and severity of the winter. So, according to this method, an all-black woolly bear actually foretells a short, mild winter. Seems like woolly bears are right no matter what they look like. I'll bet TV weathermen wish they had such a win-win scenario.

Woolly bear caterpillars are actually the familiar larvae of a species of tiger moth, the scientific name of which is *Isia isabella*. Like any other moth, the caterpillars eventually spin a cocoon and transform into their adult stage, a boldly patterned moth.

Woolly bears over-winter as caterpillars, and in October and November often cross roads and sidewalks as they search for a protected place to hibernate. Woolly bears travel pretty fast, for caterpillars – when they build up speed they can go 80 yards per hour, or about a 20th-of-a-mile per hour. This speed is useful, because the caterpillars sometimes must travel quite a distance to find a winter place safe from cold and predators.

In the spring, they leave their hiding places and, after eating a few more leaves, spin a cocoon. In about two weeks, depending on the temperature, the adult moths emerge, and soon mate.

Female tiger moths lay eggs in early summer on a variety of plants. The larvae hatch, mature, change into adults, and lay eggs again by late summer or early fall. The woolly bears we see in autumn are thus actually from the second generation of the year.

There are a number of other kinds of tiger moths, all of which have larvae with dense coverings of hair. The hairs are an adaptation to avoid bird predation. Apparently, robins and blackbirds and such don't care for furry meals.

An all-black version of a woolly bear, with red bands circling the body, is the larvae of the great leopard moth. This species feeds on plantain, and seems to be fairly plentiful. A light-colored version is the yellow woolly bear, which looks like the usual woolly bear except it is all light-colored and has hairs not all the same length.

I am not sure what you can predict looking at these other wooly bear species – but I could probably make something up.

Woodchucks

Cold weather in recent days has really got the woodchucks worried. At least it seems so. Nearly every orchard or farm field has a few of the furry knockwursts waddling around looking for a last meal before disappearing until at least Feb. 2.

In our area, the 'chucks will more likely hibernate until late March. It seems that European colonists adapted a traditional holiday, Candlemas Day, to the woodchucks. On Candlemas Day, which also falls on Feb. 2, the similar European badger was supposed to see his shadow back at home.

Woodchucks, which earned their other name, ground hog,

after colonists cleared much of their original forest habitat, hibernate as deeply as a mammal can. Their body temperature will drop from a normal of 96 degrees to 37 degrees. They will breathe only once every five minutes, while their hearts will beat about once a minute. With such a slow metabolism, woodchucks burn little of the fat they so diligently pack on in the fall. The fat is burned when they awaken in early spring, when new grass and other delectables are scarce.

A few evenings back, I sat waiting for a deer to approach my tree stand. No deer came, but the woodchucks feeding in the old orchard I watched really gave a show.

Periodically an apple fell, crackling through the branches before landing with a thump. At the "thump," four or five woodchucks raced to the sound. Whichever one arrived first seized the prize in his front paws and glowered at the others. The rest wandered off disappointedly while the lucky one feasted, sitting back on its haunches and turning the apple in his forepaws, much like we eat an ear of sweet corn.

Over the summer, woodchucks feed on a variety of greens. As any gardener knows, they will supplement their diets with tomatoes, beans, and young sprouts of almost any vegetable. In the fall, they search for especially rich foods, such as apples and wild grapes.

Before settlers cleared the forests, woodchucks were forest animals, which explains their name. They climb trees adeptly, and often do so, either for a better view or to reach food. If there is a good acorn crop, woodchucks spend much of their time in the forest gorging on the fallen nuts. Late in the season, woodchucks seldom climb; they appear so fat it's a wonder they can walk. Yet, despite the plump appearance, a woodchuck over 10 pounds would be a monster.

Woodchuck burrows vary in size and length, seemingly

dependent on the disposition of the owner. Usually there is one obvious main entrance, with a large pile of fresh dirt in front of the opening. This will not be the only entrance, however. Woodchucks depend on their burrows for safety, and usually have at least two "back doors" to run to if a predator threatens.

Old woodchuck dens are important to other wildlife, especially rabbits and foxes. Neither of the latter species is as capable a digger as the woodchuck, so both often adopt burrows. Foxes probably kick woodchucks out of their burrows occasionally. Other species that use old woodchuck burrows include skunks, opossums, snakes, box turtles, and even pheasants.

Chipmunks

The wind blew capriciously, sometimes cooling my neck from the west, sometimes cooling my face from the east, and sometimes just swirling about, sending leaves spiraling skyward.

Deer probably enjoy days like this, knowing that their keen noses will detect virtually any hunter in the forest. I enjoyed the day, too, although the errant breezes put my hopes for fresh venison on hold.

And the chipmunk scurrying about under the tree I was in provided plenty of entertainment.

Acorns rained from a huge red oak 20 yards away, and the chipmunk worked on the bumper crop constantly. One of the entrances to his burrow was under a fallen tree nearby, and he raced to and fro with his booty. The chipmunk always paused at the burrow entrance, and appeared to carefully inspect the acorn he carried. Balanced calmly on his hind legs, he turned the nut over and over in his paws, sniffing it carefully. He reminded me of a shopper inspecting peaches at the supermarket.

Most likely, the chipmunk checked each acorn for signs of rot, although I never saw him reject any acorn he got as far as the entrance to his burrow. Maybe he merely gave each a nut a last sniff before packing it away, in anticipation of a mid-winter snack.

Unlike gray squirrels, chipmunks do not store their winter supply of acorns by burying each individually. Instead, they designate one room in their underground burrow as the food pantry, and stuff it full of nuts, berries, and seeds. What goes in the pantry depends on what is available in the chipmunk's home range, which is usually less than 100 yards wide.

The pantry makes a nice complement to the other rooms in a chipmunk's "house." Other rooms are used for sleeping, for a winter bathroom, and for giving birth. If weather during the cold months is severe, chipmunks will spend the entire time in the comfort of their dens, although a warm spell may bring them out for a breath of air. A chipmunk spends a large part of his winter in hibernation, but periodically wakes up for a bite to eat.

As day turned into dusk, the chipmunk slowed the pace of his work, pausing frequently to survey the woods from the top of the fallen tree. When he was still, his striped coat blended remarkably well with the bark and moss background, an effect that increased as the sun sank below the horizon.

After sundown, the chipmunk ceased work altogether. He sat on his log in the pink light of dusk, watching the woods for danger and listening to the rhythmic calls of the other chipmunks: "chock chock chock chock."

He called a few times himself, proclaiming the log and all near it as his, and then scurried into his burrow to await another day's work.

Flying squirrels

One of the least-often seen mammals is also one of the most unique. It is active only at night, can leap more than 100 feet and feeds mostly on seeds and nuts. Give up? The animal is the southern flying squirrel.

Flying squirrels don't really fly. Instead, they soar on "wings" formed by folds of skin between their front and hind legs. The folds of skin, attached at the squirrel's wrist and ankles, provide more than 50 square inches of surface area. This adaptation makes it possible for the 3-ounce rodents to make long, gliding leaps from tree to tree with the greatest of ease.

The flying squirrel's eyes are another unique adaptation to its lifestyle. The little animal always looks startled, because its round black eyes seem about three times too big for its face. The increased light-gathering surface area provided by these optics allows the flying squirrel to move about freely at night.

Flying squirrels are much smaller than the commonly seen gray squirrel. From head to tail they measure only about 11 inches, compared to 18 or more inches for the gray.

During the day, flying squirrels den in hollow trees, usually using old woodpecker holes for their nests. They occasionally make their homes in attics or barns, and have even been known to use mailboxes for nests. A tree hole can be checked for occupancy by gently rapping on the tree with a stick. If a flying squirrel is home, it will quickly peek out with its typical, wide-eyed expression.

Like gray and red squirrels, flying squirrels are active all winter. They make several caches of nuts and seeds to carry them through the cold months. In the warm months, flying squirrels add numerous insects to their diet.

Because of their nocturnal habits, the exact status of flying squirrels is difficult to determine. Not long ago I had some living in the attic of my Alexandria Township home. Interesting though they may be, flying squirrels do not make good tenants. A good analogy might be that of a drummer who lived upstairs and liked to practice all night.

The squirrels at my place had it made, because we always had feeders full of sunflower seeds out for the birds. Their favorite was the plywood tray beneath the living room window, because it was an easy leap from the roof. We would hear scratching noises above us as we lay in bed, then a short pause, and then a loud "wacka-wacka-wacka" as the tray vibrated from the squirrel's landing. In a short time, the squirrel would scuttle his way back to the roof, no doubt to store some of the seeds before leaping down for more.

A flurry of snows

I was in a bad mood on Monday, Nov. 27. I do not remember why, but when I am in a bad mood I go out and split firewood, so that is what I was doing when I heard the first snow geese.

I heard them quite a distance off, and thought at first they were Canadas, which are a dime a dozen over Hunterdon County. After listening for a moment, I turned to my wife, Cathy, who was helping with the wood.

"They're snows, Cath."

We walked to the north side of the house and waited, looking for white birds against the gray, unsettled sky. They came right over the house, 300 hundred strong, crying in their strange, spirit voices, higher in pitch than the calls of Canada geese. The birds flew low, much lower than snows usually fly when they migrate, probably because of the stormy weather. We could clearly see the black tips on their undulating wings.

How could such a sight and sound fail to lift any grump's mood? Snow geese populations thrive, increasing every year, even though human troubles pale beside what these birds face in their lives.

Another flock of snows appeared out over the Amwell Valley; then later, another, and another. I quit splitting wood and watched. Between 2:30 and dark, almost 1,500 snow geese passed, disappearing over the Sourland Mountain en route to the salt marshes of the Jersey coast.

Their journey started last September, when the birds left their nesting grounds in the far northern Northwest Territories and Greenland. Snow geese nest so far north that in some years the warm season is not long enough for them to successfully nest. It is not unusual for most of the snow goose population to experience complete nesting failure in a given year.

The birds probably arrived on the St. Lawrence River below Quebec City in mid-October. The St. Lawrence is a major staging area for snow geese, more than 2,000 miles south of their breeding areas. Most snow geese remain on the St. Lawrence until freeze-up approaches.

From the St. Lawrence, these snow geese migrated directly across country for about 350 miles, passing over my home on the way to places like Brigantine National Wildlife Refuge, or the salt marshes on the Delaware Bay near Fortescue. One far-off flock surprised me when it circled and briefly settled on a distant field, before taking wing once again.

The geese will eventually winter somewhere between southern New Jersey and North Carolina, feeding on salt hay in the marshes and on grain in farm fields before beginning the long journey north in late February or early March.

After picking up the split pieces of oak, I went inside. I was not in a bad mood anymore. Splitting wood had not helped, but the snow geese had.

A precious place

It is a rank place, thick with weed, dense with branch, smelling yet of summer, though this will change very soon. Verdant green from without, within the place takes on hues of black bark, pale green under-leaves, and brown, trampled earth where deer have been.

A woodchuck startles and huffs off through the weeds and brush. He is a fixture here, he and five or six others, coming here from their dens on the hill, under the old barn, and beyond the fence. The place, untended these many years, overrun with wild grape and wild rose, still yields a crop.

The woodchucks, the deer, the squirrels, the coons, they all know. The apples are theirs; I share, but am here for a different crop.

The branches groan and give slightly as I climb, commenting how I got away with it this time, and who knows about the next time, but I know how tough old apple wood is, and I do not worry.

A loud thump! seems to travel across the ground, up the trunk, and through my chest. A deer ... no, wait, an apple fell, and – there! – a woodchuck races to the spot and noses around, like a beagle on old scent, until he bumps the fruit with his nose. He is on his haunches, turning the apple in furry paws, before I notice the second one, walking disappointedly off. They have been playing this game for days, this game of listening for the thump and racing to the spot.

No one can see me here, though 50 yards away a dirt lane parallels the three rows of trees that make the orchard. If I could be seen, I might not come here.

It is a precious place, this orchard, too precious to share, which is just as well. Few humans would endure the thorns, the lingering ticks, just to reach a bedraggled, ancient orchard. The apples are covered with woody brown spots, fraught with worms, and just fine with me, thank-you.

Between the chucks, the squirrels, (and the man in the tree), the deer must wonder where all the apples went, when they get here. An alfalfa field lies across the lane, and this place serves up the appetizers before the main course. I don't really expect any deer this night, though I'd like to see the 8-point; the wind is very shifty in the face of the approaching cold front. What I'd really like is to be here the day after tomorrow, after the front passes, the first day after a crisp night of north winds.

———-

You know it's the day by the thrush calls overhead, unseen shadows passing before the stars, the piping notes of the Swainson's and the thin "vree-eeks" of the gray-cheeks. You know to be at the orchard before dawn, and this is why. Standing on the lane in the dark, you shiver but are warmed by the lisps and zips and other notes binding thrushes and many other birds together as they fly. Are they kinglets? Yellow-rumps? White-throats?

Familiar, twittering wings brush past and you sense a movement in the road. A migrant woodcock, one of the first. You will later flush it, or one of its kin, as you enter the orchard.

A thin band of red, laid moments before across the horizon, begins to turn pink, though it is still quite dark. You need to be in the tree before the band turns yellow, so you crouch and ease along the path, one hand in front of your eyes guarding against branches. You no longer carry a flashlight when coming here. You no longer need one.

The first birds you see are scaling across the tree tops, chipping softly, then settling in above you. Warblers. The thrush calls are now below and all around you. A Swainson's spirals up his song – a young bird, you think, practicing for next June.

The light is now enough to see shapes and silhouettes, and a warbler silhouette lands nearby, on one of your tree's dead-and-should-have-been-pruned-20-years-ago branches. The warbler preens, and you watch as the increasing light lifts night's veil from the bird. Your hands reach for your binoculars, and then you remember you haven't brought them. Some notion about spirits being easier to detect unfiltered.

No matter, the light rises, the bird is close, and already you know it's a blackpoll. The date suggests blackpoll, and when the bird scratches his ear with a yellow foot, you grin. Blackpoll it is.

Other birds are evident now, many birds: kinglets, warblers, a few vireos in the trees, thrushes and sparrows and, somewhere, the woodcock, scratching on the ground beneath you.

The blackpoll finishes preening and looks at you – directly at you, head cocked, wondering, never having seen a human in a tree up in Quebec. Or so you think.

And you think, lots of birds today, but a little low on spirits. Or was the blackpoll saying something you could not hear?

————-

The colors span the spectrum, now, and frost coats the oval apple leaves littering the ground. I hear a thundering of wings as I approach the tree, and wonder as I climb whether the grouse will return while I am here. I hope that it will, but think that it will not.

Only one or two woodchucks linger above ground, but deer sign is even more evident. Several bucks have taken to the sassafras saplings scattered along the orchard's edge, stripping the bark from calf-high to waist-high with their antlers.

———

You are in the tree for an hour before the grouse returns, a red-phased bird. When it turns away and fans its tail slightly, you see the unbroken dark band of a male. The grouse picks at a half-eaten apple, composing a pretty picture as it feeds in a spot of sunlight on a floor carpeted by apple leaves.

A sapsucker mews softly somewhere, and when you turn you are surprised to find the bird a scant 10 feet away, on a branch arching up and away from a neighboring tree. You do not reach for the binoculars. The bird watches you with one eye, the near one, then falls from the tree and disappears further into the orchard.

You sense the deer before you see him, or perhaps some deeper part of you recognizes his footfalls before your conscious self hears them. The buck, four long points on each of his mahogany antlers, rakes the ground with his foot, then lowers his head and softly blows puffs of steam onto the leaves as he searches for ... an apple? A doe? An intruder? He moves randomly, but is getting close to your tree, and you begin to feel something tingling on the back of your neck and deep in your chest. The 8-point reaches your trail and stiffens as he breathes deeply the smell of leather and silicone and of every place you've been in the past week. The feeling melts from you, and the buck melts from sight.

———

The orchard stands silent, unpruned branches bowed with heavy snow. Yet the place still offers a crop. Rabbit trails run in all directions, and an interested fox has intersected most of them. The third tree on the left has always had a screech owl in the hole on its south side.

A few winter weeds are yet identifiable. The thistles are easy, and the narrow-leaved mountain-mint gives itself up when I

crush the dried flower head between my fingers, and breath the
fresh, wintry smell.

———————

You enter the place for the last time, dousing yourself with
snow-laden branches. One or two withered, brown apples still
cling hopefully to the trees, perhaps afraid to take the leap
which will start a new life. If you believe an apple could feel fear.

You nod to the screech owl as you pass. You would like to
stay and watch it, as it blinks at the scudding clouds. But you are
unwilling to linger, unwilling to force it to choose another roost,
unwilling to chance making the owl uneasy. If you believe an
owl could be uneasy.

The wind sends tiny tornadoes of snow crystals spiraling
across the ground, wrapping them around the rabbit-gnawed
rose bushes. A chickadee scolds softly as you climb the tree and
brush snow from your perch, then utters a few high, soft dee-
dee notes that quiet the silence and herald a gray-winged wraith
slipping through the orchard.

The sharp-shinned sets down on the limb where months
before your blackpoll preened, and takes turns glaring toward
you and the chickadee. You still your breath, hide your pulse.
You are a stone.

The wind sends another series of crystal tornadoes, the
sharp-shinned's branch waves, the chickadee scolds again, and
you can feel at once and quite clearly the spirit, breathing cold-
ly but gently on your nape. If you believe an old orchard could
house a spirit.

You believe.

Thoughts on hunting

This morning, like 20 firearm deer season opening mornings
before this one, I watched from a tree stand as light came to the
December woods. I heard a hermit thrush offer its dawn call to

the wind and falling snow, and I ached for the sound of an approaching deer.

Hunting is where I learned to listen, and I like to think I listen well, but today the deer came silently through the snow, a trotting doe followed by what could only be a pursuing buck. The binoculars confirmed it: a spike buck, small but legal quarry. The shotgun came up intuitively, as it has dozens of times before, and crosshairs followed the buck's shoulder through the brush. Falling snow hissed, a chilly breeze crossed my neck, I knew I was squinting in the too-dim light, that the shot would be forced and uncertain, and I lowered the gun as the buck and doe, shadows now, passed out of sight.

People often ask how it is that a naturalist can also be a hunter, how someone who loves wildlife can take an animal's life. This is a valid question, one that perhaps needs a book-length essay to answer.

I know that modern hunting is acceptable biologically, that regulated hunting does not threaten any wildlife species (witness the deer herds throughout the country) and may in fact be a necessary means of keeping certain wildlife populations at levels acceptable to humans.

I believe that if humans are going to eat meat, and most do, wild meat makes as much sense as beef or chicken. My family eats its meat mostly as venison, and so I try to bring home, butcher, wrap and freeze six or seven deer every year over the course of the various bow-and-arrow and firearm seasons.

I became a naturalist in large measure because I was a hunter first. I spent hours in the woods looking for rabbits and deer, but also found red-tailed hawks and gray foxes, huge white oaks – and wind in the birches. Many times, the themes for my nature writing come from my experiences in the field with bow or gun.

I don't hunt because it is fun, like football or tennis. Hunting is one of the most enjoyable things I do, but it is no game. I often say that I am both a hunter and an anti-hunter, in that I am frustrated with some of the behaviors and attitudes displayed by hunters. Too many hunters trespass, handle weapons irresponsibly, or brag abut their exploits as if a dead deer were a bowling trophy. Hunting is much more serious than that.

For me, not for everyone certainly, but for me, it would be unnatural not to hunt. When hunting, I feel like part of nature, a participant as opposed to an observer. Hunting is a connection to what is real, and when a deer approaches my stand, the unrealities of cars, computers, deadlines and paychecks disappear.

I did not kill a deer today, although I might have. Perhaps I will tomorrow. Regardless, I will be hunting, watching the sun rise, listening to the thrush, waiting for a deer. I will be hunting what is real.

Mice and men

Mouse immigration season is well under way. Immigration into the house, to be exact.

Two kinds of mice might be found in a typical Hunterdon home. One, the house mouse (*Mus domesticus*), doesn't even belong on this continent, let alone in your silverware drawer. House mice originated in Asia, spread to Europe, and were brought to America very early in the continent's colonization period. Like Norway rats, house mice were stowaways on the old sailing ships.

The house mouse is uniform gray with large and prominent eyes and ears. It evolved in close association with humans, and is almost never found away from some sort of a building. House mice eat anything a 10-year-old boy will eat, and a few things he won't. They gnaw constantly, and will shred all kinds of fabric for their nests, including fabric from furniture and clothing.

The other "house" mouse is the white-footed mouse (*Peromyscus leucopus*). White-footed mice are often called field mice or deer mice. This is the mouse who comes in for the winter. Ordinarily, white-footed mice are denizens of forests and overgrown fields, where they feed on insects, carrion, and various plants and seeds. However, in winter they are certainly not above finding a safe, warm haven in your attic, basement, walls or kitchen cupboards, and don't mind eating the crumbs you leave behind. I think that many times white-footed mice (and also Norway rats, by the way) find their way into houses because they are attracted to the vicinity by bird seed scattered on the ground by homeowners.

White-footed mice are quite attractive. As the name implies, this mouse's feet and underparts gleam white, while the upperparts glow golden brown. When full grown, a white-footed mouse might exceed 7 inches in length, including the tail.

Both kinds of "house" mice are very prolific, which is why they can quickly become a nuisance. Females give birth up to eight times per year, and each litter has four to eight young.

If white-footed or house mice become a problem, the worst thing to do is put out rat or mouse poison. Although effective, poison can be dangerous for pets and young children.

Poison also has unacceptable environmental side effects, mainly on the animals which feed on mice and rats. Poisoned rodents do not die instantly, and so can wander outside, where their weakness and unusual behavior makes them easy targets for owls, hawks, and foxes. The predators may in turn be poisoned by eating a poisoned mouse.

House cats and snap-traps are two effective alternatives to poison. Snakes also work well, but most people would rather have mice.

Three squirrels

A gray squirrel trio livened my morning by diligently ignoring me, all the while working hard on their winter quarters.

Actually, they did not ignore me, exactly. They just paid little attention to that thing leaning against the tree next door.

Now and then, one paused and stared at me, and chuckled a few soft notes of irritation. Usually, if one got started, all three would stop what they were doing and look. Two or three times, the three got themselves so worked up that they scurried up the big oak, out one of the tree's immense spreading branches, and into the knot hole that was the entrance to their den. They did the same thing, only with much more enthusiasm, when the local red-tailed hawk flew over.

After a short time, a squirrel's face and beady eye appeared at the knothole. He or she (there is no way to tell on squirrels at long range) watched me, watched the sky, watched the ground, and, since I made no false moves, eventually climbed out, followed closely by the other two.

Most likely, the three squirrels represented a family group, either brothers and sisters, or perhaps parents and young. They certainly seemed to enjoy each other's company.

The trio frequently remained on the limb for several minutes after an alarm, perhaps making sure the woods were safe again. Sometimes they played together for a bit, chasing each other back and forth, around and under the limb and in and out of the hole. Animals like squirrels do, indeed, play. The playing apparently has survival value for the animals; in the case of squirrels, it may build skills in climbing and maneuvering on tree limbs and trunks.

After playing, the three climbed down the tree and went back to work.

The squirrels expected a cold spell, for they carried load after load of oak leaves up the tree trunk and into their home, at least 15 loads while I watched. They collected the leaves close to the den tree, and carried them up the tree in their mouths. When they reached the hole, they stuffed the leaves halfway in, and then climbed in themselves.

This was the funniest part, really. There would be this wad of leaves sticking out of the hole, and then one by one they disappeared, pulled in by an unseen squirrel. The sound of crunchings and scrunchings emanated from the hole, and soon the squirrel climbed out of the hole and down the tree for another load.

Personally, I would think oak leaves are on the scratchy side for bedding material, but then I do not have a gray fur coat to keep them from my skin.

A naturalist in the city

"I drove into New York City yesterday."

"Wait a minute, Don, I must have a bad connection. I thought you said you drove into New York City yesterday."

"I did, Chris."

It wasn't the kind of thing I would typically do on a beautiful November day, to say the least. But I figure I got off easy.

The kids were enjoying the teacher's convention school holiday, and since I also had the day off, we were planning on spending a "family day" together. My wife, Cathy, asked what I would like to do.

"Anything, as long as it's outdoorsy," I said cheerfully.

My daughter, Rebecca, said, "Let's go to the mall."

She's only 7 years old. If shopping tendencies are genetic, those genes aren't from my side of the family. Going to a mall, especially so close to the holidays, makes about as much sense as willingly driving on New York City streets.

I said, "Well, since it has to be outdoorsy, we have to just go to the Nature Company and Eddie Bauer."

Cathy piped up, "Let's go to the American Museum of Natural History!"

Clearly, "outdoorsy" means different things to different people. But I actually like the American Museum of Natural History, so off we went. We took Cathy's Jeep, in case we needed to do any off-roading.

We had a wonderful time, visiting the blue whale, the Hall of American Mammals, the African mammals and, of course, the dinosaurs. My favorite exhibit, and also Cathy's, was the one with the lynx stalking the snowshoe hare. Donny, my 12-year-old, liked the rocks and minerals. Rebecca and Tim, who is 10, liked the blue whale.

We had so much fun, in fact, that we talked about spending a week's vacation in the city, and going to the museum every day. Even better (from my perspective), we also decided to go whale-watching next summer, and to someday take a safari in Africa.

I kept a wildlife list from the time we exited the Lincoln Tunnel and headed uptown. Birding from the car is something I do all the time, although it was a little difficult to watch the skies and the crazy cab drivers at the same time.

Even so, I logged an impressive five bird species: rock dove, house sparrow, starling, ring-billed gull, and herring gull. We also saw some very interesting mammals.

We probably could have found quite a few more if we had taken a walk in Central Park, which really is a good place to watch birds at least, but we stayed in the museum until its 5:30 p.m. closing. As much as I like looking for owls, Central Park in the dark didn't appeal to me. Surviving the drive out of the city was worry enough.

Oh, well. At least we weren't at the mall.

November fires

I am sprawled on the floor next to my Lab, Rachel, soaking in the warmth of a fragrant oak fire. We needed this fire, Rachel and I. We earned it.

Good wood shouldn't be wasted, so the first requirement for a fire is having a reason to make it. Our reason was a cold November Sunday spent traipsing the fields and woods of Clinton Wildlife Management Area, near Spruce Run, where Rachel chased pheasants and I watched them fly, along with the white-crowned sparrows, water pipits, and sundry other species pushed up by 70 pounds of fast-moving dog. If I walked five miles, and I bet I did, then Rachel ran 20. We're both out of shape, it is cold and windy, and when we got home we needed the fire.

It's an oak fire, as I said. The wood is hand-split, aged a year, and absolutely perfect. The only wood I'd rather have is some dense, heavy hickory. Hickories are so strong that they seldom fall down, and I don't cut down trees just to make firewood. This red oak's demise was a happy accident.

We have a reason. We have wood. We still need a little kindling, easily gathered from storm debris along the hedgerow. We look up in time to see the red-tailed hawk leave his favorite perch near the clearing, and hear his scream as he catches the singing northwest wind and pretends to migrate down the ridge. We know he's a resident, and likely will be back as soon as we are gone inside.

Other migrants move this day, however, and if we weren't so darned tired Rachel and I would climb the ridge and watch for the golden eagle I just know is coming my way, out of Canada and across the north county ridges. The clouds, the low afternoon light, and the wind's song all say golden, but we gather our kindling and leave the surmised eagle to his flight.

Reason, wood, kindling ... just a little newspaper for tinder (so I'm a cheater) and a match, and some memories to pass the time as the fire grows.

Rachel probably thinks of one or another of the day's pheasants, but my mind drifts farther back, to other Novembers colored by woodsmoke, other places, and other birds. Some brought signs of the changing season, some were signs that the season had already changed: typical November fare.

Several years ago, a November weather system out of the west brought one of the rarest birds I have seen in Hunterdon. That ash-throated flycatcher, a western stray, made braving the day's bitter winds worthwhile. Another day, in the wake of a powerful Canadian cold front, I watched spellbound as dozens and dozens and dozens of bluebirds migrated over the house we rented in Alexandria Township.

One night near Thanksgiving, a mass of juncoes thronged at my feeder, 100 strong, feeding desperately in preparation for the first of many winter storms to come.

And today there was the red-tailed, settled on his winter territory, ready for whatever and wherever the winds of winter blow.

I am sure he would build a fire, too, if he could.

What the goose thinks

It is autumn, and a wild Canada goose stands alone next to the park pond. A mature bird, the goose probably carries 12 pounds on its black legs, most of the weight in the front, in the form of once-powerful pectoral muscles for flying. These muscles have languished unexercised for some time now.

Two years and two months ago the bird learned to fly, practicing a thousand miles to the north, in Canada, where Canada geese should. Now the bird's left wing dangles lifelessly, like a 5-year-old's front tooth, and the feathers on the wing are worn and gray and shredded.

The goose lived at the park all summer. Looking at it, you would think it would be dead by now, but there you go. It has looked that way since it first arrived at the park – or, more correctly, since it was first injured. Many facts about the goose are unknown.

No one knows what happened to it. No one but the goose knows that it is not one of the local flock, but rather a migrant, a bird that chance dealt some horrible accident on the journey north to Canada and, by way of a cruel apology, dealt a brief sanctuary at the park. No one knows who to blame, or who is responsible for taking care of this little problem.

What could tear a wing like that? One favorite answer to that question is a poacher, a man with dark, beady, close-set eyes crouching in the reeds with a big gun. The geese flash over, the shot flashes up, one bird spirals to the water, its mate circles and honks frightenedly – until the big gun roars again.

"Maybe a fox got hold of it," some people suggest, imagining the burnished fur creeping through the tall grass, the swift legs rushing, the cruel teeth grabbing and ripping. Treacherous things, those foxes, vicious and uncaring.

A villain must be involved, anyway. Isn't one required in a

tragedy?

A very few people notice the high-tension lines crossing the park, only a quarter-mile from the pond. Of those who do, only two or three at most realize the most likely cause of a broken wing on a bird that heavy and strong, and that many villains are involved, and that many are at the park right now.

The public feels sorry for the goose, and wants something done, the public being comprised of lovers walking hand-in-hand over the pond's bridge and having their special moment spoiled by the sight; of moms on the way to the playground with their kids, who have to answer when little Sarah asks, "Why doesn't that duck fly away?" of people who admirably hate to see an animal in such apparent suffering; and even of a few people who know it is a Canada goose, and that it is injured, though no one seems to want to acknowledge the fact that the wing cannot be saved.

People think about the bird when they visit the park.

Many of the park regulars have called the office about the bird already. Two wrote letters to the local newspaper, catalysts for more letters and more phone calls. Some suggest assembling a big group of people and rounding the bird up, not considering that the pond is rather big and deep and that the goose is not apt to recognize or appreciate good attentions, and is even less apt to be caught by such a crew. This goose swims as well as any goose or maybe better, since it has had much practice swimming of late. A few pragmatists think a long-handled flounder net would be just the ticket for capturing the goose. People who like to watch wildlife shows on cable TV suggest rocket nets or tranquilizer darts.

Today something is going to be done for the goose, finally. It is 3 p.m. and two rangers sit in a 4-wheel drive patrol vehicle at the park entrance, watching vehicles leave and making sure no more enter the park for the next half-hour. Two other rangers are on foot patrol, asking joggers and bird watchers to kindly leave the park. The rescuers do not want any interference from the public.

By pre-arrangement, the story being told is that a potentially rabid raccoon has been seen down by the pond.

One person waits by the pond, waiting for the others to clear the area, and watching the goose.

Everyone has sympathy for the goose, even the park rangers who suffer the complaints from the public. People imagine what will happen to the goose when winter comes, when the pond freezes and snow covers the grass and the people who feed the ducks and geese in the park visit only occasionally, on exceptionally warm, sunny afternoons. When the north winds blow, they will deliver the goose rough times.

The goose amazes everyone, living this long with one wing listlessly dragging the ground. Few realize, or choose to think, that the torn wing removes the goose from the gene pool for good. If the bird's mate still lives, it is nowhere in sight. Unmated geese are not apt to feel sympathetic toward a cripple.

The goose proves that wild creatures know how to live, and how to keep living, but not how to stop. Why should they know anything else? What else is there to want when you are wild, other than to live? The goose has earned a lot of respect during its tenure at the park.

Here comes an unleashed dog; go for the pond. It is a retriever that can swim; crouch in the reeds and wait for the dog to be called off. A snapping turtle paddles through the oozy muck; swim away. The station wagon with the man wearing a hat pulls up; swim over to get bread. Night falls; tuck your head and wait for tomorrow.

There is fatigue; ignore it. There is hunger; ignore it. There is fear, and suffering, and failure.

A group of geese passes high over; call a welcome. The flock circles and continues south. Another group passes. Call. Another group. Calling burns too much precious fat; be silent.

Everyone thinks this goose will die, when winter comes, unless something is done before then.

I wonder what the goose thinks. I have to wonder, because I am the one who will pull the trigger.

About the author and the artist

When not birding, hunting, hiking, biking, canoeing or fishing – or writing about it – Don Freiday works as chief naturalist for the Hunterdon County (N.J.) Park System. His degree in wildlife science is from Rutgers University.

Don writes regular columns for New Jersey Audubon magazine and the Hunterdon County Democrat newspaper. He is widely regarded as one of the best field birders in New Jersey, although his interests cast their net across all things on, in or above the earth.

Cathy Freiday, registered nurse by trade and artist by avocation, shares her husband's enthusiasm for the outdoors. She called on her observations in the field to create the pen-and-ink illustrations for this book.

Don and Cathy explore, write, draw and share with their three children, Don, Tim and Rebecca.